The Lepers Among Us

Homosexuality and the Life of the Church

Dr. Jim Reynolds

PRESS

The Lepers Among Us
Homosexuality and the Life of the Church
by Dr. Jim Reynolds

Printed in the United States of America

ISBN 978-1-60266-933-8

www.xulonpress.com

Foreword

ᐊᐃᐧᑊᐁᐧ

I write this book from within the community, for the community and because of the community of faith. For 15 years I have been privileged to walk with men who are struggling with same sex sins. I have not had any occasion to walk with women who struggle in the same way. Yet much of what is in this book is directly applicable to women as well.

My relationship with these men has been in the common life of the Church, not in a para-church setting designed just for the same-sex strugglers. Much of the time has been spent in a house church setting involving anywhere from 6 to 15 people. Homosexual sin has been one among many sins diagnosed, confessed and forgiven.

The dynamics of God's Rule - shame-lifting grace, idol-smashing authority, life-giving Spirit and the re-socializing by new Fathers, Mothers, Sisters and Brothers - has dramatically changed all our lives. All of this happens in the common, ordinary life of real Church.

I have seen and continue to see substantial redemption within these men's lives, men who have moved from living in a gay world, full of gay relationships, to living in a new family. On four occasions I have preached the weddings of these men to women. I do not claim they live in a struggle-free or sin-free existence, but then neither do I make that claim for myself. Nor do I consider marriage to the opposite sex the benchmark of successful sexual reorientation from homosexuality. What is of fundamental concern is the new walk into intimate prayer in the Spirit, powerful covenant connection with the

Body of Christ and walking into the God-ordained ministry calling. The kingdom dynamics within a real community of disciples obliterates the dynamics of shame, detachment, disempowerment and hopelessness on these I have called "the lepers among us."

These disciples not only lead small groups at the Lake Highlands Church but are also engaged in all sorts of ministry within the church. One serves as the church administrator and leader of the church staff. Their stories are known throughout the entire church, yet they are not unique among the many and varied stories of redeemed lives through Christ.

All of us are being restored to the way of Christ. Same-sex sins are just one of many sins among us. In all respects the redemption of these Disciples is the work of God in the ordinary, plain vanilla church. The plain vanilla, basic Christian church is the most powerful force for good on planet earth. Nothing is more powerful than God doing basic Christianity in the church. It is out of this wonderful time of walking together that I write this book.

I dedicate this book to these disciples who have changed my life and vision forever: Wesley Chin, Dennis Coleman, Michael Perkins, John Cundiff, Marshall Bradley, Jay Winn and Michael Spain. I also thank Wesley Chin for his reading, editing and correcting of this manuscript. His work has always improved the book. The weaknesses of this book are mine.

Introductory Word

༺✕༻

Failure to live out the reality of Jesus Christ's presence in the common life of the Church with those who struggle with same-sex sins is a disease of epic proportions, a malignancy that spreads throughout the Body and resurfaces as the Evangelical, Bible-believing Church attempts to deal with other sin issues[1]. This failure is merely symptomatic of other, deeper issues within the body, diseases that are not so easily identifiable nor that carry the same stigma or bigotry: spiritual complacency and ambivalence, hypocrisy, unaccountability, and Biblical ignorance. There is an abundance of well-written theology concerning homosexuality, but where is the embodying obedience? I am not beginning with another Bible study because, too a great extent, we already know what the Bible says. The Lord is asking, "What are you going to DO about it?"

I have written this book out of real life experiences as a family law attorney in Fort Worth, Texas and preaching pastor for the Lake Highlands Church in Dallas, Texas. The interplay of Gospel, Church, worldly culture, Bible and Spirit constitutes a great challenge for any of us who seek to minister the Good News of God's Rule to the Church and more particularly to believing same-sex strugglers!

The entire first section of this book deals with the issue of embodiment of the Word of God in the Church. The discussion of the Scripture's teaching will come later in the third section of the book, constituting the foundation for section one's discussion of the

---

[1] When I refer to the Church in this book I am referring to the Evangelical, Bible-believing Church.

ethical issues and ministerial challenges that same-sex struggler's pose for today's Church. Section two deals with contemporary cultural challenges to a biblically based Christian view of homosexuality. It includes a look at recent historical developments, scientific research, and the moral perspectives of the new paganism. The basis for positions taken in the first section will become evident in the following two sections.

Table of Contents

The Lepers Among Us
Homosexuality and the Life of the Church

In the New Testament period, there is no disease regarded with more terror or finality than leprosy. Communal reactions were swift and resolute: lepers were to be banished from the fellowship of men. They lived their lives in isolation and were required to give verbal warning of their polluted condition by crying, "Unclean! Unclean!" As such, they were denied the simple yet essential comfort of physical human contact, making Jesus' touch of the leper in Mark 1:40-42 all the more poignant.

Although this ancient disease is no longer a 21st century reality or concern, we still have lepers living among us. Socially speaking, within the body life of the Church, homosexuality is the leprosy of our time and those struggling with same-sex sins are the lepers identified as "unclean." This book, because it addresses the issue of the Church's treatment of these precious children of God who struggle with homosexuality, must begin and end with embodiment, that is, the real life of the church.

Those who come to me confessing their struggle with homosexual sin do not embarrass me. I am embarrassed, however, by the church's refusal to openly practice Christian hospitality toward the precious people who struggle with same-sex sin. Homosexuality within Christianity points to the crisis of spiritual impotence within the "straight church."

During the last three years, I have personally preached the wedding of four young men in the church who once lived in same-sex sin. No, these men did not marry each other; they married young women. God through the Instrumentality of the whole church redeemed all of these men. They were redeemed, not by some hush-hush para-church group, unbeknownst to their local church, but by God in the real, day-to-day community that is the body of Christ.

They were especially aided by the Holy Spirit as they walked with and confessed to Christian men, thereby learning what it means to be a "real" man as illustrated by Christ. It is in the Lord's church, through real brothers, fathers, sisters and mothers, that these men can get healing. I have seen this happen right in front of my eyes. I know God does this all the time. Yet the church is often telling these people to "Stay silent. You are welcome here. Just don't say anything too specific about your sin." That is a spiritual death sentence. That is the sinful hiding of Genesis 3 and that is not the *coming home* of the Prodigal of Luke 15.

Often, the churches who study – and study the Bible – don't seem to *do* the Truth. We think we are doing something wonderful when we make a good referral; either to a professional more *qualified* to handle the situation or to a Christian based organization. At that point our "job" is done and our participation in any healing that occurs is limited to platitudes and veiled inquiries. In truth, the church is betraying Christ when all she does is refer out her work of new creation to para-church professionals. Living Waters or Exodus International can be helpful for a season, for example, but the church must be the open fellowship of LIVING WATER for ALL SEASONS!

The Hypocritical church that is so uptight about penitent homosexual sinners and so accepting of penitent adulterers is killing those who struggle with same-sex sin. Dennis, a graduate from a Christian university and full time church staff employee, battled homosexual struggles for ten years. "I always fought it alone – in secret. It didn't work." Finally, Dennis publicly confessed to his church that he was losing the battle with his sin. He was removed from the church staff for a season of recovery, yet remained in his church for a five-and-a-half year period of restoration. This was a time of confession, judgment, grace, accountability, and mutual burden bearing in his local Spirit-filled church. It led to his recovery, full restoration, and to a new life of enormous fruitfulness.

Secrecy left Dennis alone with his shame. This shame has no roots in God or in real guilt. Guilt is redeemable; shame is not. Shame thrives in a context of phony religion where the religion has no grace or mercy big enough or deep enough to root out and carry away the sin and the shame. In that instance of phony, religious superficiality, the sin remains in shameful secrecy, afraid to come out and test the grace of God in the church.

Religion fails to properly diagnose homosexuality as a sin. Instead, it diagnoses homosexuality as an inoperable monstrous cancer and subsequently closes up the patient and tells him/her to stay quiet! The church is now more a dispenser of shame to those grappling with same-sex sin than it is a dispenser of righteous judgment and restorative grace!

Churches too interested in "success", whether it is numerical growth or monetary contributions, and too little interested in being faithful to God do not allow the same-sex strugglers within their churches to publicly confess or witness. Homophobia, an irrational, unbiblical, ungodly fear of those who struggle with same-sex sin, still lives among cultural Christians. Cultural Christians are by definition influenced more by their surrounding culture than by the Christ of Scripture. Homophobia puts those who struggle with homosexuality in the same class as pedophiles. It's this bigotry that fuels the fear that the public witnessing and confessing of homosexuality might scare the "straight" families away from the church. Churches that do not believe in an active, redeeming Holy Spirit in the church simply label and damn "Once a homosexual, always a homosexual."

I have watched adulterous heterosexuals "freak out" while observing a group of men, including those who struggle with same-sex sins, confess to one another, bear one another's burdens and hug each other in the Lord. An anxious heterosexual who runs from such healthy male intimacy has more sexual identity issues than those he fears. Heterosexual and homosexual men who were reared by distant fathers and authoritarian and indulgent mothers need to relearn the nature of their masculinity – in healthy interaction with each other.

We are now running those who struggle with same-sex sins into the "gay" churches. We do it every day. We do it with our stupidity. Stupidity is the combination of stubbornness, self-righteousness, and self-centeredness that says, "Yeah, I know it's wrong but I'm going to do it anyway." We stupidly refuse to minister to the outcast, partly because of the political ramifications in the church. It became expedient politically 20 years ago to begin offering divorce recovery groups in the church, though the Bible generally condemns divorce. Today, we do not deal openly with homosexuality due to sinful prejudice, and because it is not politically expedient in the evangelical churches to do so.

Basic Christianity works in the lives of those who struggle with same-sex sins. Basic Christianity is the opposite of Adam and Eve's *hiding* in Genesis 3. But for the most part, the church is still living in sin, still *hiding* homosexuals from God and from the church. This creates an enormous amount of religious shame which helps run the same-sex strugglers into fellowships such as the Metropolitan Church in Dallas, TX. When the Church condemns sin yet offers no real hope then the only option is to live in hopelessness or pursue our human "wants" to the detriment of our spiritual beliefs and convictions.

It is a sign of the sickness of the church that we have churches for heterosexuals and then churches for homosexuals, churches for whites and churches for blacks, churches where women can minister publicly and churches where women cannot minister publicly, churches for upper-middleclass and churches for lower class poor. In the interest of *comfort* and *choice* we are dishonoring CHRIST! The church is the place of new creation and God is the New Creator. God is a God of amazing diversity contained within a still more astonishing unity. If Christ is the place where "all the broken and dislocated pieces of the universe – people and things, animals, and atoms – get properly fixed and fit together in vibrant harmonies, all because of his death, his blood that poured down from the cross," (Col. 1:20, *The Message*), then His church must be the place for the redeeming of heterosexual and homosexual, black and white, women and men, rich and poor.

We don't have choices anymore. That is, we don't get to reinvent the Church according to our biases, fears and sins. *We have been chosen!* We must submit to the authority of Jesus so that the church will remind people that Jesus lives! This is the vision of chapters 1-3 of Ephesians.

The scandal of our time is that those who bang the Bible best, who do their exegesis expertly on the "gay" Bible passages, who synthesize the theology of Scripture correctly, and who do the hermeneutical move from then till now with great discernment, do not have the guts to live out in the church what they know the Scripture teaches. They don't openly embrace their penitent same-sex strugglers and provide them the fellowship of first-class, not second-class, saints. They can't do Luke 15 – they can't eat and drink with all sinners as Jesus did, who told us not only to fellowship them but to go after them!

One of the things we still do in the church is label people homosexual. We do it even when we are not guilty of blatant homophobia. When we label someone homosexual, we have diminished their divine image by naming them according to their sexual struggle. In doing so, we banish them to the shadows. WE damn them to a special condition, which is presumptively unalterable. We do it out of spiritual laziness. When we use this label, we teach ourselves to treat these people as a special sinful class. This justifies treating them as lepers in a very sophisticated, quiet sort of way.

I have learned from thousands of hours spent with same-sex strugglers in the church that we (heterosexuals and homosexuals) have much in common. We both battle a form of narcissism, a preoccupation with the self and especially the sexual self. The "gay community" is, to a great extent, a slice of extreme narcissism committed to satisfying the urges of the sexual self above all else. The preoccupation of the gay community with physical appearances is symptomatic of this narcissism. But the heterosexual community also has its huge slice of self-obsession. In the church, we often don't break the back of narcissism in the conversion process. Many of our members still stare down in the well, looking at their own reflection until finally falling into the well to their destruction. My marriage of 40 years has never been tested by homosexual sin, but is has been ravaged at times by wild, unrestrained narcissism (i.e., self-centered sin).

Something else that both the heterosexual and homosexual "communities" share is a belief in the notion that we must live out the dictates of the "higher self." For example, if I am happy in my marriage with my wife but I meet someone that could make me happier I must "go for it." This unbridled search for happiness, chasing personal fulfillment at all costs, almost ruined my own marriage. The notion of the "higher self" is an illusion, a dishonoring of a covenant commitment. The issue of what will make me happiest has no place in the life of one who follows Jesus, carrying His cross![2]

These struggles – homosexual and heterosexual – become huge spiritual crises for us who idolize sex. Our self-knowledge and our valuation of sex has not grown out of knowing God through Jesus. Thus, for the sake of sexual gratification now, we walk away from Jesus just like the rich young man who could not imagine selling the "material stuff" he had in order to receive the Kingdom. So do we, both heterosexual and homosexual alike, walk away from Jesus when he calls us away from our self-obsessed sexual idolatries.

I could go on and on with this discussion, but suffice it to say that the dynamics of sin in my life as a heterosexual sinner are the same dynamics I hear those who struggle with same-sex sins discuss. Our discussions often focus on the meaningfulness of suffering for Christ as He walks us through repentance and new life. For all of us sexual idolaters, there is no way out of the pigpen of sin and the playpen of infantile self-centered Christianity, except the bruising way of conviction, repentance, and walking through the narrow door.

We either suffer purposefully for righteousness or we suffer stupidly for wickedness. It's time to choose our suffering! It is also time to count it all joy when we suffer for Christ's sake.[3]

[2.] Mark 10:17-31; Luke 14:25-35.

[3] 1 Peter 4:13.

The overriding theme of this book centers around the desperate need for the church to offer real redemption to those who struggle with same sex sins and calls for the church's repentance and empowerment. The church must answer the call of Christ and she must address the issues posed by those who raise biblical and scientific challenges to the traditional Christian position. If the body of Christ remains impotent and unrepentant, the homosexual struggler will remain a pilgrim – a leper - apart from the family of God.

DISCUSSION QUESTIONS

1. Why are those who struggle with same sex sins treated as social lepers in many churches?
2. What is the underlying significance of hiding the same-sex struggler from the Church?
3. In your opinion, what is homophobia?
4. What is inherently wrong with labels such as "homosexual?"
5. In what ways are heterosexual temptations similar to those of homosexual strugglers?
6. Have you ever had an in-depth conversation with anyone who struggles with same-sex sin? If not, why not? What are the barriers?
7. What place does suffering have in the life of a believer? Discuss the distinction between Suffering for righteousness and suffering for unrighteousness.

Embodiment – the Lord's Test!
Living Out the Truth Now!

Paul might have put it this way:

"If I do exegesis with the skill of a surgeon and discern the theology of the Bible with prophetic insight but refuse to nurture our same-sex struggling Friends in the church, I am a self-righteous gong and a Bible-banging cymbal!"

"If I adroitly move from then to now, demonstrating with breathtaking brilliance the authority of the scripture's witness for now, but refuse to confess my own sins to same-sex strugglers while giving them only good referrals to para-church helpers I may be pleasant, but I am offering absolutely <u>nothing</u> of Christ to my brothers and sisters."

"If I don't bring my same-sex struggling friends into the open-air, fully lit, <u>middle</u> of the church, but instead urge them to stay quiet on the edges, I have become a minister of the Devil's shame, and nobody gains anything!"

Lets look at a series of questions that expose the critical need for the embodiment of the Word within the Lord's church!

"What decisions should the church make in response to homosexuality? How should the witness of the New Testament be embodied in the life of the church?" These questions challenge the entire church.

If we don't do the truth, we don't know what the truth means! Right reading of the New Testament occurs where the Word is embodied and lived out in real people. Knowledge of the will of God <u>follows</u> the community's submission and transformation. Until we see the text lived, we cannot begin to conceive what it means! For example, how often do we hear the confessions and/or testimonies of those being liberated from same-sex sins? Until we do, we do not *know* what the New Testament texts mean in today's church. The most crucial task facing us is the formation of communities seeking to <u>live</u> under the Word.[4]

"What place does someone have in the Lord's church who struggles with same-sex sins?" The place is one of *welcome* along with all of the other imperfect penitent members of the body of Christ. It is absolutely essential that homosexual strugglers live in a community of faith that renounces all unbiblical, unrelenting, ungodly shame. The church has been guilty of ministering a whispering, embarrassed shame. This must stop. By the power of the cross and <u>through the presence of the Spirit, this sin should be confessed openly</u> as one among many sins.

Furthermore, the labeling must stop. We are all children of God – Disciples of Christ. Intimate, powerful relationships with the same and opposite sexes must occur. God's redemptive change occurs in this type of spiritual environment! The church is too often leading her homosexual strugglers into "gay" churches, because she does not provide a community; too often she provides shame, discrimination and fear. God's judgment (Romans 2) is on the church for her unfaithfulness in these matters. Homophobia is not only sinful it is discriminatory! God challenges all of us, whatever our sexual preference may be to repent and reshape our identities in conformity with the Gospel. Same-sex strugglers within the Church often reveal a gross immaturity among heterosexual believers who have no vision of themselves as ministers of God's redemptive presence.

"Is it appropriate for Christians who have a homosexual preference to participate in same-sex erotic activity?" No. Despite the smooth illusions of the media, sexual gratification is not a sacred

---

[4] Richard Hayes, <u>The Moral Vision of the New Testament</u>, (San Francisco, Harper Collins, 1996), page 401.

right, and celibacy is not a fate worse than death (1 Cor. 7:8-9, 25-40). It is no more appropriate for believers to persist in homoerotic sexual acts than it is for heterosexual Christians to persist in sexual acts outside of or in lieu of marriage. At this point the church must confess her inconsistency. We wink at divorce and remarriage. We wink at pre-marital heterosexual intercourse in the church. The answer, however, is not in becoming even more inconsistent.

Gary, Richard Hay's friend dying of AIDS, wrote the following shortly before his death:

> "Are homosexuals to be excluded from the community of faith? Certainly not. But anyone who joins such a community should know that it is a place of transformation, of discipline, of learning, and not merely a place to be comforted or indulged."[5]

I would elaborate on Gary's remarks by adding that for all those who do not struggle with same-sex sins the community must also be a place of transformation, discipline and illumination. Those believers who don't know how to love those who struggle with same-sex sins need transformation every bit as much as any person struggling with same-sex sins.

"Should the church sanction and bless homosexual unions?" No. There are two possible ways for God's human creatures to live lives of faithful discipleship: heterosexual marriage and sexual abstinence. The issue here is the consistent embodiment of spiritual authority. *By what or whose authority do we do otherwise?*

Does this mean that persons of homosexual orientation are subject to a blanket imposition of celibacy in a way qualitatively different from persons of heterosexual orientation? The answer is not simple. Paul understood celibacy as a charisma, but he did assume that those lacking the charisma were free to indulge their sexual desires inside marriage (1 Cor. 7:8-9). Homosexually oriented persons are in the same situation as a heterosexual who would like to marry but cannot

---

[5] Ibid

21

find an appropriate partner (*and there are many*).[6] This is for both a *disciplined and costly obedience*, while we <u>groan</u> for the redemption of our bodies (Rom. 8:23). Difficult, costly obedience is part of authentic Christian existence, which confronts us with the gospel imperatives while challenging and frustrating our "natural" impulses in countless ways. This costly obedience must be surrounded by a compassionate, intimate community of faithful supporters.

Many of the advocates of unqualified acceptance of homosexuality, in and out of the church, seem to be operating with a simplistic view of man that assumes "whatever is, must be good." They have a theology of creation but no theology of sin and redemption. Furthermore, they have a radical "now" view of life in Christ that equates personal fulfillment with sexual fulfillment and expects sexual "salvation" NOW! Paul's portrayal of human beings as fallen creatures in bondage to sin and yet set free in Christ for the obedience of faith would suggest a rather different assessment of our sexuality, looking to the future resurrection as the place of bodily fulfillment. Thus the now and the not yet of the end times looms as the crucial question that divides the traditional position from those who would revise it.[7] Yet in the church since we have often taught a "you can have it all now" life in Christ for the greedy, the gluttons, or the unfaithful, our words to the same-sex strugglers often possess no salty authority!

"Should homosexual Christians expect to change their orientation?" Yes. The transforming power of the Spirit really is present. The Lord God is changing lives. Witness the testimonies of thousands who have been healed and transformed into a heterosexual orientation.

First of all, the deliverance needed for both heterosexuals and homosexuals is not first a deliverance from a sexual orientation but a *deliverance from the idolatry of sex and its attendant sexual lust*. This change is desperately needed throughout the church. This seems to be the spiritual condition reached by Gary near the end of his life:

---

[6] <u>Ibid</u>., p. 402

[7] <u>Ibid</u>

"Since All Saints Day, I have felt myself being transformed. I no longer consider myself homosexual. Many would say, 'Big deal. You're forty-two and are dying of AIDS. Big sacrifice.' No, I didn't do this of my will, of an effort to improve myself, to make myself acceptable to God. No, he did this for me. I feel a great weight has been lifted off me. I have not turned 'straight.' I guess I'm like St. Paul's phrase, a eunuch for Christ."[8]

Gary's change is the Lord's deliverance from false identity and from an attendant lust!

The second change includes an awareness of the relative unimportance of genital sex. I mean unimportant when compared with the "weightier matters." Marva Dawn, a physically disabled though extremely able teacher says it well:

"Is it fair that I who once was extremely active and skilled in sports am denied the physical pleasure of running and playing because of a crippled leg? Is it fair that loving music as profoundly as I do, I am denied the sensual pleasure of hearing it well because my deaf ear constantly rings? Is it fair that severe limitations prevent me from enjoying beauty and make me unable to do the reading that I love and must do for my work? To be denied sexual fulfillment (as I also was for many years) does not seem to me to be such a great suffering. Though I am passionately in love with my husband, I would gladly give up sexual happiness to get my vision back. (You see, dear readers, I am easily as guilty of making an idol of visual pleasure as others might be of the idolatry of sexual pleasures. We are all sinners in rebellion against our creator!)"[9]

---

[8] Ibid., p. 403

[9] Marva Dawn, Sexual Character (Grand Rapids, Michigan, Eerdmans Publishing Company, 1993), p. 108

Dawn's words contain a liberating truth seldom heard anywhere in this culture in which a fourteen billion dollar pornography industry pumps out images day and night. These changes, liberation from sexual idolatry and the debunking of the supreme importance of sex in America, should occur as the church speaks "truth in love" to her members, leading them to a radical counter-cultural maturity. Sex is one of God's fragile gifts – not a devil and not a god!

Sexual idolatry is personified in the 45-year old man who leaves his wife of 20 years for another man. This bisexual behavior, probably better labeled "sex obsession," exemplifies Paul's analysis in Romans 1:18-32. The narcissism (radical self-centeredness) of a therapeutic culture drives us, making the fulfillment of our sexual selves absolutely compulsory! Romans 6:1ff describes the death of narcissism in the life of the believer. This death to sin is too often soft-pedaled. Cultural Christianity panders to our narcissism, telling us Christ will give us the highest pleasure and prosperity. Costly discipleship must be preached and lived in the church. "If any man would come after me, let him deny himself ..." (Mark 8:34).

Clearly change should be expected, but the change in homosexually oriented people in the church should be only a tiny part of the change going on in the church. When the entire church is not in continual transformation, how can we ask homosexuals to change? If the church is just a pleasant but not a powerful place of redemptive connecting, the church has no help for her members who struggle with same-sex sins.

Sexual orientations and behaviors are not immune from the healing powers of God. We expect this change to occur. We live in the power of the Spirit. We are not bound by a psychological or biological determinism. The gay lobby wants to question the testimonies of those who have changed their sexual identities from homosexual to heterosexual. But the changes are well documented through the week-to-week church and para-church ministries such as *Living Waters Sexual Redemption in Christ* program.

Though Living Waters is wonderful, the Church is God's real redemption program. It is in the living of life in the Spirit and the forming of strong, healthy same-sex and opposite-sex relationships in the community of Christ that we are set free. I see this happening in the church where I am being liberated. But all too often it is not yet happening within the wider church – only in the para-church – only in the programs quietly run by the church. This backwardness, this spiritual immaturity must be confronted and renounced. This "spiritual stupidity" that secretly sends the homosexual strugglers away to get healed runs through churches. The church is still too often the place of self-righteousness, the place where more sin is hidden than any place on earth. When the church really practices a life together as Bonhoeffer described it, LIBERATION will reign in the middle of the church and not just in a para-church run by a few professionals.

"Should persons of homosexual orientation be ordained to ministry in the Church?" Biblically speaking, there is no distinction between clergy and laity. All of us are clergy.[10] The battle line is not drawn at the point of ordination to professional ministry! The Church has no authority to teach a double standard – one for "clergy" and the other for "lay people."[11] The church has no special rules to exclude from ordination the greedy or self-righteous or lustful. A person who struggles with same-sex issues, seeking to live a life of disciplined abstinence, would clearly be an appropriate candidate for any and all ministry. This assumes the requisite gifts and maturity for ministry within this man or woman. I know ordained "professional" ministers who struggle with heterosexual lust issues, yet these men have served in ministry for years. The issue was always the extent to which these men lived in liberating discipline and accountability for their actions, words and fantasies.

At the present time there are a few evangelical churches where a man with a homosexual propensity who lives in disciplined abstinence could minister. However, there are more churches that would not "call" such a person to their church. Thus churches often pass by single people, like the late Henri Nouwen, the great Catholic teacher, spiritual director and priest who lived a celibate life of

---

[10] This issue must be revisited in the Church. Passages such as Ephesians 4:11-16 indicate that all of us are being equipped for the ministry. See Paul Stevens, The Other Six Days (Grand Rapids: William B. Eerdmans, 1999), pages 5-9.

[11] For example, the only difference between the qualifications for elders and deacons in 1 Timothy 3:1-12 is elders should be "apt to teach."

disciplined abstinence while struggling with a homosexual propensity. The Church is the loser when she makes such fearful immature decisions.

Dennis, the man referenced in chapter one as being overcome by homosexual sin, stepped away from his staff position for a season of restoration. He remained in the Lake Highlands Church during the period of restoration and now serves as a paid church administrator for the church. He has also gotten married to a Christian woman in the church, fathered a child, and is a shepherd-leader of a home church.

This restoration within the whole Church, not a secret parachurch, has taken 10 years and is ongoing. But Dennis' restoration is no different from mine and many others. The redeemed brokenness on the Church staff where I work is apparent, humbling and a powerful witness to the effectiveness of the Good News of the kingdom rule of Jesus, Lord and Christ.

"Should the church support civil rights for homosexuals?" Yes and No. Yes, to the extent that we should not single out homosexual persons for malicious, discriminatory treatment in the workplace, the courthouse or the neighborhood. This in no way endorses their behavior any more than it endorses the behavior of the heterosexual live-ins who have the same civil rights. The answer is no, however, in the sense that I do not support homosexual marriage or the recognition of homosexuals as a protected social class.

The key issue in the link with civil rights is the issue of choice. Is homosexuality something you are, like being black, elderly, handicapped or female, or is it something you do, like adultery, polygamy, or incest? But what if that question can only be answered on an individual basis? Then there is no discernible class under which one might seek civil rights protection. Yet, it still makes no sense to me to discriminate against same-sex live-ins while excusing the heterosexual live-ins next door.

The issue of custody of children should be determined factually, asking what is in the child's best interest. Parenting factors on both sides must be weighed. I would not rule out a homosexual parent, though I consider the homosexual factor a substantial negative. The other parent could be a convicted felon or beset with an addiction that negates their viability as a parent; homosexual acts are not the only sins in the world.

The issue of same-sex marriage licenses goes to the issue of whether God ordains such marriages. Scripture at no point envisions homosexual marriages. Biblical marriage always includes two elements: covenant and the polarity of the sexes (Genesis 1, 2 and Matthew 19:1-9). Therefore, I don't support any same-sex marriage legislation.

It is said that Malcolm Muggeridge, the late English journalist, became a disciple of Christ after touring a leprosarium run by Sister Theresa. Muggeridge had for years believed that humanism – belief in the best of human nature - was the most powerful force for good on earth. After his tour of a facility built and run to care for and provide a good death to lepers, Muggeridge declared that humanism does not possess the spiritual or moral energy to run such an enterprise. It was Sister Theresa's witness to Jesus at the leprosarium that led to Muggeridge becoming a Christian.

Today, when the "homosexuals", the lepers of our time, are ministered to and fellowshipped openly and redemptively by the whole church, when the whole church touches and practices hospitality, and when the whole church mediates healthy guilt and forgiveness instead of homophobia and shame, then the world will see Jesus and many will be led to name Jesus as Savior and Lord who now give Jesus no respect!

This chapter has briefly focused on several embodiment issues. The next four chapters will now discuss ministry to same-sex strugglers within the common every day life of the Church. These sections will not focus on civil rights issues or the wider social and legal issues regarding homosexuality. The primary focus will be the basic every day life and ministry of the local church to same-sex strugglers.

In my judgment, the failure of the evangelical Church - Churches that still claim to believe in the classical Christian doctrines such as the inspiration of Scripture, the incarnation of God in Christ, the substitutionary atonement and the resurrection of Christ, etc. – to bring same-sex strugglers into her common life is a great tragedy. At worst this tragedy points to a spiritual bankruptcy and at best to a gross immaturity within the Church. We are called to a <u>Church-wide repentance</u>!

Evangelicals who act as if the Biblical Word will accomplish the Lord's mission but who say little about the Spirit or the Church are helpless when called to assist same-sex strugglers. We must rediscover the vision whereby the <u>entire</u> community is empowered and mobilized for ministry by the Holy Spirit of these last days!

DISCUSSION QUESTIONS

1. Discuss "Until we see the text lived we cannot know what it means!"
2. Discuss the church's need to repent and mobilize for ministry to those struggling with same-sex sins. Discuss how shaming, labeling, stereotyping and homophobia are counterproductive to any real ministry attempts.
3. Discuss Marva Dawn's witness regarding both the importance and relative unimportance of sex.
4. Discuss the debunking of sex as an idol as well as the redemption of the sexually self-centered self.
5. Discuss the power of repentance and transformation in the life of the church as well as the homosexual struggler's place within the church.
6. Discuss: should people who struggle with same-sex sins be considered for ordination to ministry?
7. Do you see some personal frustration inherent within the "now and not-yet" within all believer's lives, until He comes? Discuss the relevance of this for all of us.

A Typical Tragedy

(A Call to Repentance)

The tragic story within this chapter of a Christian leader hiding his struggle from his <u>own church</u> personalizes the issues. These are Kingdom and People issues. I criticize some of the man's testimony. But the greatest issue posed by this story is the <u>leadership void</u> in the Church. What would you do as a Church leader or Church member if this man came to you and told you his story? Would you bury him, hide him, shoot him, or maybe take his class away from him? Or would you shepherd this man and the Church into maturity?

Is this man more dangerous than we heterosexual pastors who continually must discipline our minds propensity to fantasize the attractive women in our churches? The issues come to rest in our laps! What are we going to do: politicize or pastor? Read on!

On March 11, 2003, <u>Christianity Today</u> published an article by an anonymous man, a follower of Jesus, who struggles with his propensity for homosexual relationships while living as a faithful husband and father.

"I am a business executive, congregation president, youth group leader,

athletic coach, happily married man for more than 25 years, and proud father of a couple of teenagers. Oh – and I'm gay."[12]

---

[12] Author Anonymous, "No Easy Victory" Christianity Today, March 11, 2003, page 50.

This man goes on to describe his Christian upbringing and his struggle with homosexuality from childhood. "While my high school peers were bragging about their heterosexual exploits, I was trying desperately not to have the homosexual encounters that my nature inexorably seemed to draw me towards."[13] At age 19 this man became a disciple of Christ and much about his life changed. He recovered from depression, got his drinking under control, quit smoking, and straightened out his sexual life enough to begin a healthy relationship with a woman he later married.

During the last 25 years he has tried counseling, therapy, prayer and healing to become heterosexual in his mind. "But for all my trying, all I've managed to do is control the behavior manifestations of my sexual orientation. God has given me the power to live a fulfilling heterosexual life, together with the grace to live with the fact that I'm still homosexual."[14]

I disagree with his assessment that he is homosexual because he "almost daily battles" homosexuality at a considerable psychological cost. He gives himself no credit for what he does. He gives weight only to what he feels. He is mistaken. Every heterosexual man, to one extent or another, daily battles with lust, fantasy addictions and/or romance addictions. I don't know any heterosexuals who after being born again began living a life of pain-free, struggle-free sexual purity. That doesn't mean these heterosexuals are what they struggle against, just as this same-sex struggler who also functions as a husband and father is not what he struggles against! He is certainly not a homosexual, that is, his identity is not his sexual preference.

The statement, "I am homosexual" is more a statement about loneliness, about his struggle to diagnose himself all by himself. The shame within the loneliness, the inability to get the issue out into the common life of the Church sets him up for a missed diagnosis. The struggle in loneliness, his palpable suffering sense of separation, has helped him label himself in an inaccurate and nonredemptive manner!

---

[13] Ibid.

[14] Ibid. page 52.

I certainly do not discount this disciple's pain or struggle, for as he says in the article, the journey of marital faithfulness has <u>been much tougher</u> "without the support of friends or a caring Christian community." He has no idea the help and blessing he has missed all these years!

As the writer says, he offends the liberals because he believes God intends for him to live in heterosexual monogamous fidelity, but his experience of a grace that saved him but didn't fix him or make it easy for him to live a "straight" life offends the conservatives who preach and demand "a clearer victory" over his sinful nature. Much of our preaching rhetoric does not resonate with this man's story or the story of most in the Church.

The tragedy of this story resides in the following words: "Why haven't I told my story to my Church friends? Why is my identity anonymous? Because despite all the claims by my heterosexual friends to 'love the sinner but hate the sin,' I do not trust them."[15] He goes on to say that if he revealed his struggle to his friends they not only wouldn't let him be the youth-group leader or their son's coach, they wouldn't continue to be his friend. He correctly perceives a special indulgent dispensation being given to young male heterosexuals by the same people who would consider any homosexual acting out by any Christian an utter abomination.

His reasons for not trusting the Church are all probably based on the reality in the Church. Unfortunately, he probably reads most of his Church correctly. Yet even so, his continual act of distrust is <u>sin</u>! The heterosexual community is full of people who cover up their sexual lust and/or behavior, all the while claiming they cannot trust anyone. We often refuse to live in authenticity, to "speak the truth in love" and it is sinful behavior. This type of posturing deception is at the heart of the sickness within the Church. This type of Church culture contributes to the same-sex struggler's distrust, but it does not excuse his action of telling no one. Does he live in a Church where some intimacy and transparency exists? If he does, he will be built up in the Lord by bringing his sin into the light of real fellowship. But he in cooperation with the Holy Spirit must do it! Begin

---

[15] <u>Ibid</u>.

31

with two or three brothers or sisters; let the leaven work within the Church!

MUTUAL TRUTH TELLING

Paul, in Ephesians, admonishes believers to "put off your old self which is being corrupted by its deceitful desires" (4:22). "Therefore, each of you must put off falsehood and speak truthfully to his neighbor for we are all members of one body ... Do not let any unwholesome talk come out of your mouths, but only what is helpful for building others up according to their needs" (4:25,29). He goes on to say, "Let no one <u>deceive</u> you with <u>empty</u> words because of such things God's wrath comes on those who are disobedient" (5:6). At the very heart of a redeemed life is a redeemed <u>mouth</u>! When our mouths hide in silent deception, refusing to confess (i.e. tell what God would tell if he were talking) we speak empty words. We engage in falsehood. We do not speak truthfully to our neighbors. Our talk, though anesthetized, is unwholesome and is not helpful to anyone.

The heterosexual youth-group pastor who struggles with his fantasy life, but who is <u>walking</u> in obedience is not disqualified, but only if he lives in authentic truth-telling and mutual confessional burden-bearing within the body of Christ. Confession is an absolutely necessary burden bearing for those of us who still commit sins (1 John 1:1-5). When the heterosexual begins confessing and discussing it results in greater understanding. We realize our sin is every bit as dangerous as any same-sex sin. We can then begin to hear the confession of our same-sex struggling brother or sister and more properly discern them. We will also find ourselves confessing our sins to brothers and sisters who battle same-sex sins.

The Holy Spirit will illuminate the truth-tellers and the truth-receivers in the Church to properly weigh and discern what they are hearing. The knee-jerk homophobic response has nothing to do with the Spirit's presence and leading. The issue is where is the Holy Spirit leading us? The Spirit is leading us into the unbreakable bonds of the Family of God; the one-anothers, such as "confess your sins, one to another," "Forgive one-another," and "Wait on one another," that knit us together as enduring soul mates. It is there that we must begin taking risks – all of us! Authentic, powerful churches must replace the phony, pleasant churches! The Spirit will do this as we take God's risky path of truth-telling and God-trusting. This is the via dolorosa, the way of suffering Jesus walked with us to the cross!

As the anonymous writer in Christianity Today says of those like him, "Ours in no easy victory. It would be a whole lot easier if our churches would try to understand and accept those like me who claim victory nonetheless."[16] This lonely disciple accurately envisions the enormous assistance the Church could and should be giving those who struggle with same-sex sins.

I was saddened by the tragic anonymity of this writer and by the fact that his whereabouts were described as the "western half of the United States." The apparent unwillingness to even disclose to the reader the state this man lives in spoke volumes! This anonymous man bemoans the rejection of a Church he has never trusted as he hides in the "western half of the United States." These dynamics serve as living parables of the same-sex struggler in today's evangelical church.

A CALL TO THE CHURCH

At the present time the following qualities of Christian community are notably missing in the Evangelical Church: normal contact with and understanding of the same-sex struggler by the Church, any significant understanding of the trap into which a homosexually inclined person feels himself thrown, any community of responsibility for dispensing God's judgment and grace. The Church has not typically allowed the issue of homosexuality to take its place with other offenses on Paul's list. The same-sex struggler is a "they" or a "them." We do not identify with them.

But are those who struggle with homosexuality any more deviant than the rest of us? What about the sin of a sociopath pastor who uses his station as pastor to sexually abuse those he is counseling?

---

[16] Ibid.

Or the distraught young father compulsive to some kind of public exhibitionism? Or the seventeen year-old boy who keeps a diary of his seductions of eighteen teenage girls while competing with his best friend for a "score" of twenty-one females? Or the fifty-year old man who counts the number of times the word sex is mentioned in the Sunday sermon while during the week he sexually fondles and harasses his female employees? Or the married couple who talk with their friends about the possibility of getting pregnant but who in actuality have not had sex in 10 years? Or the heterosexual who commits adultery? Or the men and women who would much rather masturbate while looking at a screen of sexual images acted by professionals than have sexual relations with their real mate's imperfect body-soul, skin, and mind? Or the secret wantonness (intentional, relentless lust) of those who have made secret careers out of sexual unfaithfulness, while never disclosing their behavior to their wives? Or the man who leaves his wife and three children to fulfill his "highest self's" desire for completion with his "true" soul mate? Or the "normal" lying and cheating done by the "normal" people in the church?

The stories go on and on! These are the stories of the "straight, normal" people in the Church! They are endless, ad nausea! No wonder Jesus said to the hateful self-righteous Pharisees, "He that is without sin cast the first stone."

If we are not living in denial we will accept the same-sex struggler as one of us, for we too are blind, lame and broken. In many instances the brokenness of the "straight" church is even greater than that of the same-sex struggler's. At least most of the same-sex strugglers I know acknowledge to me their sin struggle. We know the diagnosis! A stronghold of denial, deception and delusion corrupts many of the "straight" sinners! They don't know the diagnosis!

We must grow beyond our self-righteousness. We must become and become known as a community of responsible involvedness! We must love sinners as Jesus did:

"Now the tax collectors and sinners were drawing near to hear him, and the Pharisees and scribes murmured, saying, 'This man receives sinners and eats with them.'" Luke 15:1,2

Then Jesus tells three stories - the lost sheep, the lost coin and the lost boy – to defend his <u>involvement</u> with the social outcasts. The Church <u>seldom</u> has to tell these stories to defend herself because seldom do we openly and responsibly involve ourselves with the outcasts!

As one Christian recently told me, "I don't hang out with homosexuals." This same person talked at length about the Church's need for the Holy Spirit. But he did not seem to realize that the Gospel of Luke describes the Holy Spirit moving Jesus to "hang out" with and minister to the outcasts. Yet when it came time for this man to identify with and minister to the social outcasts of our time he wanted no part of it! He did not seem to understand that the Holy Spirit is at work redeeming all of us together in One Body under the cross. This man was interested in what the Holy Spirit could do to heal his Mother's cancer, but he was not interested in the Holy Spirit using him to touch sinners and hang out with them. This type of "what has God done for me lately?" Christianity knows very little of the Jesus in Luke's Gospel and the Acts of the Holy Spirit!

We will have to become and become known as a community of *real guilt*. Only as we forego our own self-styled spectatorships, only as we confess our common guilt as homosexuals and heterosexuals, is there redemption for any of us!

"There is no one righteous, not even me; <u>there is no differ-ence</u>. For all have sinned and fall short of the glory of God." Romans 3:10, 22, 23

The Church has to become and become known as a community of grace. A Christian struggling with a homosexual identity usually has never experienced the shocking unmerited favor of God in the Church. In the community of responsible involvedness, which is a community of guilt and grace, we see grace at work when we bridge the "them" and the "they." Fellowship of the repentant homosexual struggler as a broken brother or sister no more constitutes a moral compromise than does love for a repentant alcoholic constitute acceptance of drunkenness as a Christian lifestyle.

"For it is by grace you have been saved through faith – and this is not from yourselves, it is the gift of God – not by works so that no one can boast." (Ephesians 2:8-9)

LISTEN TO THE STORIES

The Church must listen carefully to the brother or sister who struggles with same-sex sins. There are no cookie-cutter people. There are no identical stories. The telling of stories offers tremendous insight into those who struggle with homosexual sins. The radical self-centeredness of our time as well as the idolization of sex has led many of us, regardless of our sexual preference, into destructive godless behavior. Our sexual identities are partly the result of our being sinned against. The heterosexual whose Father taught him to fornicate with women but not to respect them or whose Mother taught him that sex is dirty also suffer from sexual identity confusion.

Many disorders and sins contribute to sexual identity confusions: a distant, abusive Father; a sexual predator who rapes a skinny, effeminate thirteen year old; a Mother who emotionally smothers her son while pushing him away from his Father; a house devoid of physical touch or verbal blessings between Mother and Father; brutal punishment for normal sexual attractions; a terribly competitive unfriendly and sometimes cruel dating system; masculinity defined entirely by football, basketball and baseball; a life in which there has <u>never</u> been an attraction for the opposite sex. The experiences are legion. All of our stories need to be told in <u>detail</u>, heard by fellow loved ones and brought into the circle of spiritual illumination and discernment. This listening in the Spirit goes far beyond psychiatric insights.

Within the telling of stories we begin to make important distinctions between homosexual identity (orientation), homosexual acts (behavior), homosexual lifestyle, and homoerotic impulses. Each person we talk to who struggles with same-sex sins is unique. Some have never "acted out" but are concerned about their homoerotic impulses. Others have "acted out" occasionally but have never lived with a same-sex partner. It is <u>very important</u> to hear the full story, making discerning distinctions.

NO POWERFUL COMMUNITY – NO REDEMPTION

The Lord God is continually creating a people for His name, whether it is Israel or the Church. We cannot over emphasize the singular importance of the Church for the redemption of everyone, including the homosexual struggler. The lack of an ecclesiological (Church) perspective within the evangelical church renders her impotent in regard to the redemption of same-sex strugglers. Books that are otherwise very helpful exhibit little understanding of the importance of the Church. For example, Christopher Wolfe, who recently edited the book, <u>Safe Sex Matters</u> – an excellent collection of essays on homosexuality – asks, "What should homosexuals do?" He says, "First, young homosexuals in particular should seek out counseling to explore the possibility of therapy to reverse their orientation."[17]

Wolfe is wrong. They first need to seek out the Church and become *known* within that Church body. Stop the secretiveness. Throw themselves on the <u>fullness</u> of Christ in the Church where the long-term redemption lives! Professional therapy can also be a significant component of the redemption, but it is <u>secondary</u> to the real, healthy, permanent redeemed relationships to be found within the Church. The Church – her leadership – must covenant to provide a powerful, safe place for those who struggle with same-sex sins.

Wolfe does say that it is imperative that defenders of traditional norms regarding homosexual acts convey their admonition and affection to homosexuals who strive to live lives of self-control. Wolfe goes on to say, "But, inevitably the most important and credible source of exhortation to live according to right moral norms will

---

[17] Christopher Wolfe, "Homosexuality in American Public Life" <u>Same-Sex Matters</u>, Christopher Wolfe, ed. (Dallas, Spence Publishing Company, 2000), page 22.

have to be homosexuals themselves who can provide support and friendship to each other in their efforts."[18]

Again, I believe Wolfe is wrong. He represents the conservative Christian notion that Christians don't really need the Church. They just need a para-church group that is full of people who all struggle with the same thing. That is not Church! The notion of the Fullness of Christ in the whole Church, where all the members minister to one-another in the Spirit, is nonexistent. Same-sex strugglers desperately desire the unconditional love of the "straight" Church. Their typical shame issues cannot be effectively addressed by restricting their open and honest relations to only those who struggle with the same issues. Same-sex strugglers must allow themselves the blessing of having the grace of God mediated to them from those who struggle with other sins as well, and vice versa. It is then that all of us realize we truly belong – whatever our struggles as imperfect children of God. When the Church functions as a healing community where understanding, forgiveness and love flow, the Church is the perfect environment for dealing with same-sex issues.

Again and again in home church gatherings in which Wesley, Michael or Dennis have confessed their sins related to homosexual acts I have found myself confessing to them the dynamics of hetero-sexual lusts and acts. Our discussions reveal a common narcissism, sexual idolatry, a love for sexual and romantic "highs" and a frustrating incompleteness in all of our lives. The telling of these stories draws all of us into the wider circle of struggling – laboring redemption. The support and friendship is very wide and very deep.

Mario Bergner, author of Setting Love in Order, a man who was once a practicing homosexual but is now redeemed by the Lord Jesus, believes there is no healing for same-sex identity struggles apart from entering into *non-erotic same-sex relationships*. But it was also the Body of Christ where he came into right relationships with women. Martin Buber's word, "All real living is meeting" suggests to Bergner that unless we are willing to encounter (meet) people and work through our relational difficulties, we will never be

---

[18] Ibid., page 24.

healed enough to truly love. Basic Christian fellowship plays a huge role in <u>transforming</u> our heart's images of men and women.

Bergner speaks of the power of an authentic holy man on his life as he began walking out his salvation.

> "Simply by being a <u>faithful Christian,</u> he became a sacramental channel through which God's healing flowed into me. This whole man in Christ left a far deeper influence on me than what he said. My heart began to be resymbolized that day. The old distorted symbols of confused masculinity were disengaging from the story line of gender identification in my deep heart. Now <u>new images</u> of whole masculinity began to find their rightful place there."[19]

This is the work of God within the whole Church.

DISCUSSION QUESTIONS

1. Do you know of anyone in your Church who is living a similar tragic story?
2. Do you know of anyone within your Church body that has openly confessed their struggle with same-sex sins? If so, what are you doing to help them? If not, how do you think your Church would respond to such a confession?
3. Would the man's story described in Christianity Today be the same in your Church? Why? Why not? How do you know?
4. Do you believe that "straights" are often just as sinful and disordered as any same-sex struggler?
5. Do you think "straight" members of the Church can minister to "gays?" Why or why not?
6. Do you think people just need the Spirit and the Bible but not the Church? How has your Church ministered to you as a recovering sinner?

---

[19] Mario Bergner <u>Setting Love in Order</u> (Grand Rapids, Baker Books, 1995), page 76.

Church – Be Healed, Grow Up, and Follow Jesus

☙❧

In order for the Church to be the Church for same-sex strugglers the character and the culture of the Church has to change. Basically we have to find out together what our lives in Christ are really about! Only the Lord Jesus can tell us! The paradox is that we don't have to get stronger; we have to get weaker. We don't need to do something significant. We need to do some very "insignificant" things. We don't need to inflate. We need to deflate and it will hurt.

We are permanently weak and don't know it. But within this weakness we can realize a strength that comes from somewhere else! Then we stop being afraid of real people with real sins, including same-sex sins. So lets get on with it!

BE HEALED!

If we are to minister to same-sex strugglers we must be healed within the new community of Christ. We don't get healed and achieve a level of maturity apart from Christ and his new community. Our healings are every bit as miraculous and hard fought as are the healings of same-sex strugglers. We too must learn to (1) accept ourselves as God's dearly beloved creation, (2) receive God's forgiveness and the Holy presence, and (3) give God's forgiveness to those who have hurt us. This will happen within Spirit-filled authentic community. It won't happen in hiding, masking and game-playing within the Church.

Heterosexuals who have confessed their lusts, adulteries, and pornographies within the Lord's community, received his blessing and equipping and walk in his redemption as <u>imperfect</u> children of God, <u>can</u> minister to same-sex strugglers. Those who have hid all their lives, acting as if all is well, putting the fig leaf over their genitals as did Adam and Eve, will not minister to same-sex strugglers.

Most game-playing heterosexuals are unnerved and/or terrified of same-sex strugglers. They live in homophobia, a godless terror of homosexuals, a stereotyping of them as a class of special revolting degenerates. The typical homophobic is full of unresolved guilt, anger and fear regarding their own sexuality. They usually suffer from an ignorance of the Biblical teachings regarding sexuality, including what the whole Bible says about homosexuality. I have seen men who were chronically unfaithful to their wives and who typically envisioned sex with any woman in images that degraded women, "freak out" when hearing the story of a same-sex struggler. The homophobic "freak out" was more about the sick "straight" guy than it was the sick "gay" guy.

It is the sick-sinful "straight" guys and ladies in the church that need to get on with their redemptions so as to resolve the guilt, anxieties, shame and lustful images that now render them impotent to minister to anybody's sexual brokenness. All of this calls leaders to pastor their sheep by discipling them, not entertaining them. Hiding behind the Bible and looking at the backs of heads in churches, week after week, year after year, won't get it done.

It is the spiritual community that "restores those overcome by sin in a spirit of gentleness." (Gal. 6:1ff) It is not just the pastor; neither is it a few professionals who specialize in "homosexual ministry." <u>It is the whole Church</u>. Only within real fellowship can any of us receive the full blessing of the Lord's face shining upon us. Only within <u>real</u> fellowship, week in and week out, can we be healed and walk out our callings.

GOD USES NOBODIES

John White, a Christian psychiatrist, in his great book <u>Eros Redeemed</u>, puts his finger on a huge issue within the Church regarding sexual healing issues! He notes that God yearns with a fatherly yearning to lead us away from our tendency to sin. He wants to make us like Christ. To do this, He not only uses repentance and prayer as a means to that end, but He also uses the people of God as a channel by which His grace comes to us. The huge issue is whether we are humble enough to <u>receive help</u>!

2 Kings 5 tells the story of Naaman, a supreme commander for the Aramite forces who was stricken with leprosy and desperate for a cure. In his desperation, he looked for help from Elisha, a prophet of Israel. Israel at that time was in decline and Aram was a great nation. Naaman had to show humility as both a commander asking a lowly prophet for help and as an Aramite asking for help from an Israelite on whom he looked down! His pride was further battered when Elisha <u>refused</u> to see Naaman and merely sent a servant to him to instruct him to wash seven times in the miserable little Jordan River. It was <u>unthinkable</u>!

As White reflected on this scripture story of Naaman he thought of his psychiatric and ministerial pose. He was always counseling and praying for others. He was a <u>helper</u>, not someone needing help. He was comfortable in the role he understood. If White were to seek help it would have to be from someone higher up in the hierarchy of helpers and White believed that there were few who qualified.

It never occurred to him that someone "lower on the scale" could minister to him. He was Naaman waiting for an important person to heal him. White's theology was sound. While theoretically he may have agreed that the Holy Spirit *could* use <u>anyone</u> to help and heal him, in White's mind it was highly unlikely that this person would be someone younger or less experienced than himself.

White's long life in Christ, however, has taught him that God <u>is</u> using "nobodies" to heal the "somebodies."[20] The threshold of our desperation must go beyond pride and encompass humility; our

---

[20] John White, <u>Eros Redeemed</u> (Downers Grove, Illinois, 1993), pgs 239-241.

hunger to be healed must <u>overpower</u> our pride. As a pastor, theologian, attorney, and therapist I have been helped by professionals, the writings of theologians and by an instance or two of professional therapy, but for the most part the people of God have helped me. Again and again in authentic community, the Spirit-filled people of God have been the instruments of the help and healing I needed and still need. These are people who do not have the degrees and professional memberships I have hanging on my walls. The issue is <u>pride</u>. Professional detachment from the people is destroying the effectiveness of pastors and psychologists every day. We detached professionals too often tend to <u>disempower</u> the Church. We teach the Church that in order to "get help" we too must detach from the Church and find a professional. We strongly imply that the "average member" could not possibly minister.

I can begin in God's power, to listen and discern the fact that I am just as broken as my broken brother or sister. When I read Andrew Comisky's <u>Pursuing Sexual Wholeness</u>, a Desert Stream Ministries guidebook written primarily for same-sex strugglers, I am struck by <u>my</u> need for the <u>same</u> ministry. I am aware of the similarity between this sinner (me) who struggles with opposite-sex sins and my brothers and sisters who struggle with same-sex sins. Heterosexuals suffer from a lot of macho-gender confusion, rampant narcissism (relentless self-seeking) and all sorts of sexual addictions. We too desperately need to become more faithful Disciples of Christ.

My sin, though I've never had a same-sex temptation in my life, is every bit as serious as any same-sex struggler's. We heterosexual sinners are responsible for the multiple millions of aborted babies of the last thirty years – not the "gays." We heterosexual sinners are responsible for the tens of millions of fatherless children in America, children we conceived, but then neglected - not the "gays!" We heterosexual sinners are responsible for the staggering divorce rate of 50% among heterosexual couples – not the "gays!"

"Let every mouth be stopped and the whole world held accountable to God." (Romans 3:19)

A preacher of 35 years, recently caught in sexual sin but now living in penitent holiness, told me that he could not find authentic burden bearing and confession among the paid staff or elders at his big church. They were all too busy calculating the political cost of hanging out with this "tainted" preacher. What he did find in the Church were three non-descript guys who had for years been battling sexual addiction sins with whom he met on at least a weekly basis to confess, share his burdens, bear their burdens and generally be of assistance in restoring one another with spiritual gentleness. If this pastor maintains <u>humility</u> before the Lord he will be healed among and through the instruments of the Holy Spirit and the <u>Body of Christ</u>!

How many of us are too proud to be healed by the Church? How many of us refuse to be healed except by a reputable professional or not at all? Clearly professionals have a significant place, but <u>long term healing</u> is going to happen when the people of the Church dip seven times in the dirty, muddy waters of the Jordan River, giving up all pride! Then we in turn will have something to share with the "lepers" in today's church, for we are also lepers. We will come out of the closet of our own arrogance to openly love all the "lepers" who seek healing.

When Christ revealed our sinfulness to us we asked in desperation, "What must I do to be saved?" We repented of our sins and were baptized by a servant of Christ. When a servant of Christ buried us in water Jesus was treating us the same way as Elisha treated Naaman. Our baptisms were <u>humility tests</u>! If we passed the test at our water baptism, have we since <u>forgotten</u> what that test taught us? Do we now stand up in pride, forgetting how we got here? Clearly pride, highly subtle and nuanced, silently strangles and separates us!

In Christ we all got in on an amazing torrent of Spirit and Grace. All of us in the dirty Jordan River, the sexually immoral, idolaters, adulterers, male prostitutes, homosexual offenders, thieves, greedy, drunkards, slanderers and swindlers! (1 Corinthians 6:10) "And that is what some of you were. <u>But</u> you were <u>washed</u>, you were <u>sanctified</u>, you were <u>justified</u> in the name of the Lord Jesus Christ and by the Spirit of our God." (6:11) And so a great washing, a great declaration of our holiness and innocence has come on us and shaped us for this very moment!

We come in together by an astonishing act of God. We remain together in utter transparency and authenticity as redeemed children. There are no "lepers" now. *All of us were lepers once.* Now we live lives hidden with Christ in God. It is an affront to my brother or sister in Christ who battles same-sex sins to label them "lepers" and not label myself a "leper." If they get labeled I get labeled! We are one in Christ - all of us. That means that a former self-righteous racist can now be ministered to by a former drug addict or former gay liberationist. Our sin struggles don't categorize us nor should they limit us to ministering to others outside of our particular struggles. Rather the fact that we both agree on the DIAGNOSIS and THE CURE and have received THE CURE dominates everything! I am helped by everyone who has been washed, made holy, and made innocent! Not just by a few hand picked saviors that specialize in my addiction of choice.

The capacity to effectively minister to one another is dramatically diminished if self-righteousness has not been diagnosed and cured. Yet self-righteousness, perhaps the greatest sin addiction besetting the Church, continues to go undiagnosed. "Homosexuals" get diagnosis and cure while the self-righteous have little if any conviction. The self-righteous believers typically sense no need for deliverance from self-righteousness. Self-righteousness always strives to makes a nice appearance, appearances being the key issue and concern. The focus is my "goodness" though I claim to be saved by Christ's righteousness. If I am saved by an amazing salvation transaction in which Jesus took my sin on himself and placed God's righteousness on me, then I should only brag about Christ, nor should I "spin" my confessions. As I recover from being a self-righteous jerk, an arrogant racist, or a wanton (one who makes a career out of lust) pornographer I give up my pride and begin maturing into ministry with and for others.

MATURITY

The Church has at least four purposes and progressive steps: (1) a nursery for newborns, (2) a hospital for the wounded, (3) a training, teaching and evangelizing organism, and (4) an army in spiritual battle with the powers of hell. If we do not practice discipleship within the Church while moving through all of these steps, we will never be and become known as a place of healing and restoration for same-sex strugglers. The newborns and the wounded (but not yet healed) typically do very little ministry. God calls us to move on out of steps one and two into the training and spiritual warfare of three and four. It is there that we mature quickly!

We have a chronic problem of immaturity within the Church. Discipleship courses just don't rank in the top ten of felt need urgencies in the Church. And so we endlessly pander to felt need crises while not helping individuals do the painful work of "following Christ." Following Christ <u>matures</u> us into helpers very rapidly. Maturity, consequently, also tends to shrink our <u>felt needs</u>!

People who shop for churches and hop from church to church every three to four years <u>never</u> mature. <u>Religious consumerism</u> breeds a self-centered immaturity in the Church that wants nothing to do with ministry to real specific sinners with real specific sins! The immature always trying, but seldom trained, refer the church lepers to professionals or para-churches. When we don't train members and don't expect our "average" member to "restore such a one with a spirit of gentleness," we disempower them for ministry. We then have an army of superficially pleasant people who do not believe God can minister powerfully through them to same-sex strugglers or to anybody else! The phrase "Men who are spiritual" in Galatians 6:1 is not referring to an <u>elite</u> group of people in the Church. It is referring to those who have the <u>Spirit</u>, i.e. <u>all of us</u>! Then we are functioning as a mighty army in spiritual battle, trained and taught!

DISCIPLESHIP NOT FULFILLMENT

Jesus is the goal of discipleship; personal fulfillment is not. Jesus said, "Follow me." Therefore when Christian same-sex strugglers make <u>perfect</u> heterosexual fulfillment the goal, we subordinate Christ's call to a sexual identity ideal. All of us become increasingly whole as we follow him. But no follower of Christ should identify perfect sexual fulfillment with discipleship or mature redemption.

Second, neither heterosexual nor homosexual strugglers can expect to experience a complete absence of spiritual struggles in this lifetime. We live between frustration and fulfillment, all of us. We live out the "Now and the Not Yet" of the Kingdom of God. That means continuing homosexual temptations, but that also means an identity change, substantial healing and the living of a new life in God's healing power. Therefore, what homosexual as well as heterosexual strugglers can reasonably expect is to become whole enough in this lifetime to sustain fulfilling heterosexual relationships. This includes the capacity to relate intimately but non-erotically with the same sex and the freedom to encounter the opposite sex as a desired counterpart with interest, not fear or distaste.[21]

The same-sex struggler in the Church may be filled with many doubts because he or she still struggles with thoughts of a same-sex lover. The notion that unless I am 100% liberated, I am not redeemed is a lie! But this lie can be most effectively exposed through conversations in Christ with members of the same sex who struggle with <u>heterosexual</u> lust. The presence of the struggle does not mean that we have not been liberated; It means I am still prone to sinfulness, even while living in a new identity and new life, substantially redeemed in God's power. Heterosexual strugglers must be telling <u>their stories</u> to brothers who struggle with same-sex sins. As we read scripture, pray and tell our stories we begin to more truly discern what is going on in our lives. John said that if we say we don't commit sins we are liars (1 John 1:1-9). If we act as if we don't commit sins we may cause our own brothers to stumble and fall, deceived by our <u>own plasticity</u>. Our new identities are brand new and enduring, though we may commit or think about committing the old sins from time to time.

---

[21] John Harvey, <u>Truth About Homosexuality</u> (San Franciso, Ignatius Press, 1996), p. 99. The actual words in this quote are Andrew Comiskys from his book <u>Pursuing Sexual Wholeness</u> (Lake Mary, FL, Creation House, 1989), p. 187-188.

Remember, all of us become increasingly whole as we follow Christ. We see, but not with 20-20 vision. We love, but never perfectly; we can do all things, but we are weak. We live in the "Now and the Not Yet" of the Kingdom of God. We await the perfect fulfillment of the Kingdom.

NO DISCIPLESHIP WITHOUT FELLOWSHIP

Discipleship, for anyone, was not intended to be lived out without fellowship (Koinonia-sharing). Discipleship without fellowship contains an abusive dimension. It reminds us of Jesus' words to the Pharisees in Matthew 23 regarding those who bind heavy loads on the people's backs, but do nothing to assist them in bearing the load. When we read scripture together, tell each other to do what it says and then never assist one-another in bearing the load, we sin against God.

Superficial posturing speech is unwholesome falsehood. I am referring to a church culture of chronic unwholesome, superficial falsehood whereby all of us, strong and weak alike, <u>deceive</u> one-another. This is <u>religious</u> abuse! The first people who will be held accountable for this are <u>church leaders</u>. Church leadership sets the tone; plastic leaders lead plastic people. Plasticity in leaders is a form of religious abuse. Plastic leaders have no clue what to do with same-sex strugglers.

When Christ is received as Lord and the Spirit baptizes us, believers are described in Acts as being of one heart and mind. This is what the <u>energy</u> of the living God does in a community where the Spirit of God is released. This means that it doesn't take a year or even six months to <u>share our lives</u> with brothers and sisters among the *Spirit immersed*. It can happen within a matter of hours or days or weeks. Where the Spirit is <u>not</u> being quenched or manipulated people grow up fast and get knit together quickly.

DISCUSSION QUESTIONS

1. Discuss the healing necessary to overcome homophobia.
2. Who do you allow to help you and why? Discuss this in light of White's comments.
3. Discuss, "If same-sex strugglers are lepers then I am a leper."
4. Who can help restore those overtaken by sin?
5. Discuss the four purposes of the Church.
6. Discipleship, not 100% struggle-free life, is the goal. Discuss.
7. "Discipleship without fellowship is abusive." Discuss.

Church as Healer

People who must hide their struggle and have already labeled themselves homosexual haven't even begun to receive and give God's forgiveness and are consequently not being redeemed within the Church. This chapter points to the ongoing ministry of the Church regarding the healing of all of us, including same-sex strugglers. This chapter touches briefly on several huge issues that should be addressed by a healing Church: practicing the presence of Christ, self-acceptance, forgiveness, the healing of memories and false identity labels. It's time for the Church to teach on these matters, but it is even more crucial that a healing Church <u>embody</u> what she teaches!

There is no such thing, strictly speaking, as a homosexual. There is only a person, created in the image of God, who is cut off from some valid part of himself. God delights in helping us find that lost part, - affirming and blessing it. So it can also be said of heterosexuals. There is no such thing, strictly speaking, as a heterosexual sinner. There is only a <u>person</u>, created in the image of God, who is not serving God with their whole life. God delights in helping us *integrate* our longing for God, heterosexual and homosexual alike, with our sexual desires.

All of us long to personally know together as joint members of the Body of Christ the words of Colossians 2:9,10, "It is in Christ that the complete being of the Godhead dwells embodied, and in Him you have been brought to completion."

THE PRACTICE OF THE PRESENCE OF CHRIST

Healing for all of us who believe is achieved and sustained by the presence of Christ. Believing God is present as promised is the discipline of calling to mind the truth that He is with us whether or not we can see or sense Him in any way. This awareness of God's presence scatters the dark cloud of shame that besets same-sex strugglers. Christ lifts shame that is too heavy to carry and that makes living the life of a disciple impossible. The Church is called to remind her members of this great work in Christ. Furthermore, the Church is called to release the Power of the presence of Christ in the life of all her members, including same-sex strugglers. Otherwise we "tie up heavy loads," but we ourselves are not equipping these strugglers to carry the burden of obedience to the King. We perpetrate spiritual abuse on same-sex strugglers by tying the heavy loads of the Kingdom on their backs, but telling them to stay quietly concealed in the Church. We offer same-sex strugglers the status of spiritual stepchildren, if that! We quench the practice of the presence of Christ by stifling these people's confessions in the whole Church.

How can I practice the Presence of Christ in a Church that will not acknowledge *my* presence?! On the one hand Christ delights in me. On the other hand, the Church is ashamed of me. This ungodly inconsistency alienates the same-sex struggler from the Church, devastates the process of sanctification by calling into question their identity as a saint and denies their innocence as a justified sinner.

If the Church, wherein lives the fullness of Christ, embraces the penitent same-sex struggler as the Father received the rebellious son in Luke 15, the Presence of God is lavishly extended and released on this child of God by the celebrating Church! Throw a party in his honor; invite the entire Church! Do not HIDE this child!

The practice of the Presence of Christ must occur in the life of the same-sex struggler. For only in Christ's presence is the healing of the separation. Otherwise, chronic shame and guilt in our minds distance us from God. For many in the army of the chronically shamed there is never a bright, shining homecoming day but only clouds, drizzle, and cold wetness, day after day. This separation has already been bridged by the Cross of Christ and by the coming of the Holy Spirit into our bodies. This is our calling now – to <u>live</u> in this Presence. But the calling is to live this Presence within the community of faith, the Family of God where we are "built up" into maturity in His Presence.

We do battle against the phallic god and the current exaltation of the instinctual, a bowing down to the dark gods in the blood. Therefore, we must wage the battle with all the spiritual armament at our disposal. A Church that treats same-sex strugglers as step-children is not <u>mediating</u> the Presence to her members. As Leanne Payne says,

> "Therefore those that hold to the traditional Biblical view concerning both the sinfulness and the healing of homo-sexuality ("Such were some of you") are looking hard for <u>pastoral</u> answers, and when they do not see them, they cry out, 'Where are they?' To cry out for pastoral answers is to cry out for the power to <u>heal</u> the lame in spirit and soul."[22]

Leanne Payne's book <u>Restoring the Christian Soul</u> discusses three barriers to healing: (1) failure to accept ourselves, (2) failure to forgive others, (3) failure to receive forgiveness. The discussion in this wonderful book walks out in considerable detail what I briefly discuss here as a part of the continuing ministry of the Church.

SELF-ACCEPTANCE – WHAT IS IT?

Self-acceptance does not rest on an <u>image</u> of myself as a nice, good, person who never did anything wrong on purpose. This approach does not allow for much <u>truth</u> within our field of vision. Self-acceptance does not run from honesty; it <u>rests</u> on it! Yet we tend to fold into denial when looking at the brutal truth about ourselves. Only the humble acceptance of myself as fallen but now <u>justified</u> by <u>another</u> who is my righteousness is the BASIS on which I can accept myself, learn to laugh at myself, be patient with myself, "and then, wonder of wonders, be enabled for at least part of the time to <u>forget</u>

---

[22] Leanne Payne, <u>The Broken Image</u> (Grand Rapids, Baker Books, 1996), page 33.

myself."[23] "Humble yourselves – feeling very insignificant – in the presence of the Lord, and He will exalt you. He will lift you up and make your lives significant." (James 4:10, the Amplified Bible)

Romano Guardini, Catholic philosopher-theologian, in his essay "The Acceptance of Oneself" writes, "The act of self-acceptance is the root of all things. I must agree to be the person who I am. Agree to live within the limitations set for me … the clarity and the courageousness of this acceptance is the foundation of all existence."[24]

Working through to this self-acceptance, affirming the real me before the real God, is no easy task. Unaffirmed men and women abound. The abused are legion. Many have been hurt by cruel religious perfectionism. And so it is that as the Body of Christ we minister the RIGHTEOUSNESS of God to one-another.

This ministry, though crucial for the whole Church, remains at the center of the same-sex struggler's redemption. It attacks the homosexual identity, which has been smeared all over our body-souls. Our self-acceptance recognizes our identity as children of God, not as homosexuals. Our identity is not sexual. Neither does it center in what we struggle against. It centers in what the Lord God has done for us in Christ. When we receive the Lord's RIGHTEOUSNESS, we also come out of denial and acknowledge *all* of our sins. But our sins do not *identify* us. The Lord's intimacy with us teaches us that he has received us into Himself, but he also calls us out of our sins. We respond to His reception of us by turning our lives to Him in wonder, gratitude and repentance! We now confess our sins to Him, never playing the liar, knowing that our sins, brought to Him in repentance, do not separate us from Christ. As we receive ourselves on His terms, we confess our same-sex struggle, but we now know that we are not homosexuals. We are beloved *Children of God*!

We teach this, talk this in our conversation, and pray this into one-another all of the time, breaking the chains of a self-hating identity, an identity born out of our greatest struggle. Our identity should and must be in the God who made us!

---

[23] Leanne Payne, Restoring the Christian Soul (Grand Rapids, Baker Books, 1991), page 51.

[24] Ibid. page 32.

RECEIVING AND GIVING FORGIVENESS

Clearly, same-sex strugglers desperately need to receive and give the forgiveness of Christ. The reception of the forgiveness of Christ is at the root of all healing. It involves moving out of denial, the inability to name the sin and to acknowledge "the snake wrapped around our persons." Clearly the same-sex struggler cannot be liberated from the shame and guilt of his or her sin apart from the liberating Grace of God that washes huge waves of God's grace and Spirit over us. We must receive the astonishing truth: "By grace you have been saved through faith. It is not of yourselves. It is the gift of God." (Ephesians 2:8)

One day I was standing on the beach in Tofino, Canada in Pacific Rim National Park, looking out into the vast Pacific Ocean, reading a plaque full of information regarding the Pacific Ocean. The Pacific Ocean, it declared, covers half the surface of the earth, constitutes three-quarters of the earth's ocean water and at it's deepest depth of 30,000 feet plus is deeper than Mt. Everest (29,000 feet) is high. This enormous body of water, though it dominates the surface of the earth, does NOT COMPARE to the heights, depth, width and length of the love God revealed to us and poured out on us through Jesus the Christ, our Lord (Ephesians 3:14-20).

If the Church is going to be the Lord's alternative sub-culture for redeemed sinners, she must drown in this ocean of God's grace. She must declare, "Not I who live but Christ lives in me." At present, the sin of self-righteousness stifles the Spirit. Self-righteousness, the deceptive ability to focus on myself and my righteousness while judging you in your comparative unrighteousness, separates us and is much too prevalent within the Church. Thus the sub-culture too often looks more like a Church for Pharisees than a Church for redeemed outcasts! Couple this sin with the sin of control, and you have a sub-culture that sucks the life right out of people. Our insecurity feeds our desire to control the life of the Church. Self-righteousness and control must be drowned by tidal waves of grace upon grace upon grace!

This means that unforgiveness quickly becomes a much more insidious, dangerous poison than almost any other sin. And yet self-righteousness and a controlling spirit mask this gross evil, always blaming a more sensual sin!

Take for example the following story whose facts have been altered slightly but is based on a very recent tragic story within the Church:

A man discovers his wife has been secretly involved in watching lesbian pornography for the last 10 years of their marriage. She is convicted of her sin, confesses, repents, and begins walking in mutual accountability with her Church. Months and months pass, then a year. The husband refuses to stay in the same house with his wife. He also refuses to be reconciled with her, though they have four children. It is ALL her fault, he mistakenly declares.

As time passes, one then two years, and then a tragic divorce, it becomes clear that the biggest spiritual issue in the marriage is not the wife's sexual sin, but the husband's inability to confess his own sin, receive the forgiveness of God and then forgive his wife. In this instance the husband's sin dynamics hovered around a horrendous, self-righteous controlling spirit that sucked the freedom and joy out of the family. His Mother had been, by his own admission, the "worst control freak ever," yet he declared that but for his wife's sinful passivity he would have never become a controller-manipulator.

Therefore, since he was only a victim, but not a sinner, he had no sins in the marriage to be forgiven of and therefore had not received the amazing grace of God, did not live every day in the PACIFIC OCEAN of His love and thus had NO MERCY to extend to his wife. This monstrous unforgiving spirit made a divorce inevitable. Tragically, a story very similar to this occurs inside a Church every day.

The pockets of resistance to the grace of God in the Church disturb and often obliterate the healing dynamics of Jesus the Healer within His own body. This man's sin, more diabolical than animal, more Pharisaical than Pagan, reminds me of the oppositional controlling Pharisees who dogged Jesus every step leading to the cross. The lady caught in the act of adultery could be told "Go your way and sin no more" but these controlling self-righteous Pharisees could not be told "Go your way and sin no more." Why? Because they had no conviction of their horrendous sin – they failed to receive with child-like gratitude the grace God sought to pour into their shriveled, self-righteous hearts!

C.S. Lewis said it better than anyone when he said,

> "The sins of the flesh are bad, but they are the least bad of all sins. All the worst pleasures are purely spiritual; the pleasure of putting other people in the wrong, of bussing and patronizing and spoiling sport and backbiting; the pleasures of power, of hatred. For there are two things inside me, competing with the human self, which I must try to become. <u>They are the animal self and the diabolical self</u>! The Diabolical Self is the worse of the two. That is why a <u>cold, self-righteous</u> prig who goes regularly to Church may be far nearer to hell than a prostitute. But, of course, it is better to be neither."[25]

When we are challenged to forgive others, the depth of <u>our forgiveness</u> is challenged. We can easily sing songs other people wrote on Sunday morning about "Amazing Grace, that saved a wretch like me" but when faced with the challenge of forgiving one who has sinned against us, leaving us bleeding and bent over, we may discern our own shallowness! As I live in the presence of God who has forgiven me for the diabolical and the animal and I internalize that forgiveness every day, giving glory to God, I am living in a huge ocean of God's grace. When called upon to forgive, I have the <u>resources</u> to forgive! That means I have the resources to do for another what has been done for me – a clean, decisive, total blotting out and carrying away the sin I committed so that it is no longer <u>between us</u>!

This work is an <u>art form</u> that Disciples of Christ walk in. For us, it is more a <u>path</u> than a <u>completed</u> moment. But we must get on the path and become very good at it! The disconnect between the songs we sing about "Amazing Grace" and all those pious words about the grace of God making us white as snow and the challenge in front of us to forgive the adulterer, the pornographer, the controller,

---

[25] C.S. Lewis, <u>Mere Christianity</u> (New York, Macmillan Publishing Co., 1945), page 94-95.

the abuser, the disrespectful, the drunk, the homosexual must be bridged by a practical day-to-day awareness of the debt I owe to the one who by GRACE saves me every day.

WE must forgive because of who we are and because we will die if we don't. The act of forgiving should not come as a surprise. We shouldn't whine about it. We are called to forgive. We are called to wage the peace. This peace becomes a climate, an ecology in which everybody breathes the clean air, drinks the fresh water and bathes in the light of the Kingdom.

Jesus' teachings including his parable in Matthew 18 regarding the man who was forgiven a $10,000,000 debt, but who refused to forgive a $10 debt remind us of the importance he placed on the spiritual obligation we have to forgive, to reconcile, to be healed of the bitterness, brokenness and rage of the past. Clearly this is at the heart of the healing of all of us, including but not limited to the same-sex struggler.

HEALING OF MEMORIES

We have thus far argued that the whole Church must be a safe, powerful place for same-sex strugglers to live and breathe. The Church must not create new relational, significance and security issues for the same-sex struggler. It is within a community of spiritual equippers that the practice of the presence of God can occur because the same-sex struggler's presence is acknowledged along with all of the other God-seekers!

The Presence of God gives us the security of forgiveness and sonship in Christ. "You are all sons of God through faith in Christ Jesus." (Galatians 3:28) One of the deepest manifestations of forgiveness is the healing of memories through the instrumentation of the Holy Spirit who ministers to us the healing work of Christ.

One of the characters in the 2003 movie "Open Range" says (paraphrase), "We can't stop thinking about what we want and what we've done long enough to figure out what we should do now."

We must be healed of the past – what we've done and what's been done to us! Only the living God within us, present in us by the Holy Spirit, can heal us. We begin now by *affirming the presence of Christ* now and at all times in the past, including the moments we were devastated by sexual abuse, rejected, abandoned and those times we reacted by sinning. This presence contains within it the seeds of our healing.

Saul of Tarsus murdered Disciples of Jesus before he was converted on the Damascus road. Later, on two occasions in Acts, Paul – renamed by Jesus – tells the story of his early murderous ways, but not as a way of groveling in guilt. Rather, as a testimony to the amazing electing love of God within Paul's life. This confession has now become his enduring testimony (Acts 26:1-24; 22:1-21). There was early on a period of repentance, healing, prayer, and preparation for Paul. It took time to even begin to comprehend the calling and the healing that began on the Damascus road. Paul's memories were baptized by the Spirit into the grace and power of God. His memories were not obliterated. They were healed!

Healed? Yes, healed. (1) They no longer tortured him with guilt. (2) They no longer infected his life with poisonous images. (3) They no longer imposed an identity on him. These memories had been swallowed up by the life of God within Paul.

Augustine, the great church Father (354-430 A.D.) who had early on lived an immoral, wasteful life exclaimed in his confession, "Great is the power of memory."[26] But Augustine writes as one redeemed knowing our memories lead us to the amazing Creator and Redeemer of our minds. "Truly you dwell in my memory, since I have remembered you from the time I learned of you, and I find you there when I call you to mind. Behold, you were within me, while I was <u>outside</u>."[27] Many of our memories are of what we did <u>outside</u>. The Lord's deep healing goes to those memories <u>outside</u>. For as Augustine knew, "You were within me" there.

Imagine, that is, see with the eye of faith, the Lord present there when you were abused or when you humiliated yourself in sin! Remember, the Lord's forgiveness of sins includes the deep healing of your poisoned, traumatic, humiliating <u>memories</u>. These events, whether our sins against God and others or others sins against God

---

[26] Augustine, <u>The Confessions</u> (New York, Doubleday, 1960), page 246.

[27] <u>Ibid</u>., page 254.

and us have tortured our memories for decades. We have sometimes on a daily basis rehearsed these events. These events have <u>defined us</u>! We have given a "spin" to our sins and our wounds, but we did it apart from the Healer of our lives!

The fact that we do not remember God's presence at these events and neither do we see God working any good out of these events indicates that repentance, a turning to the Lord and the invoking of His presence on our memories is <u>long overdue</u>! It is time to seek the Lord among His friends and invoke His Holy Presence on the past!

Our memories – the bitterness, rage and shame – are overwhelming in their power to destroy our lives. But how long do we focus on an abusive Father or Mother? I am looking at some 40, 50 and 60 year old people every Sunday morning who are not healed yet and who may not want to get healed!

When we become healthy, vibrant organisms, alive in Christ's presence, healthy tissues begin to surround the diseased tissue. Healing attacks shame, bitterness and rage, replacing them with forgiveness, peace and joy. We discern that we are not the sum total of our wounds and sins. We are Spirit-filled children of the risen King! Our lives, now filled with praise and hearing God's call, move into the great purposes of God for each of us. The wounds remain. But we are no longer sick, <u>infected</u> and swelling with poison. We walk with a limp. It's true! Don't trust anyone in the Church who does not walk with a limp!

Clearly, there may at times need to be a good Christian psychologist helping us uncover memories, but for the most part the mature Body of Christ can do the following together:

1. Affirm the presence of Christ over the one to be healed, declaring, "There is no condemnation in Christ."
2. Help one another remember the event or events. Developing the time contexts is crucial.
3. Begin praying for the healing of these memories. This involves more than one prayer because of the many dimensions of the event.
4. This includes, by faith, seeing Christ there and affirming His ability to work good into your life as a result of this evil. Your

ability to <u>see</u> this work will depend on your present relationship with our redeemer. Hasn't God done <u>indescribable</u> good by using the tragic sin in our lives to teach us of His grace and power? Paul and Augustine are just two examples!

5. We must practice pastoral discernment and follow up as we pray with and for one-another. We continue this work together for a season until the work is done!

LABELING AN IDENTITY

The following scenario and ensuing conversation could be played out a hundred different ways: a teenage son or daughter comes home from their first year at college and proclaims to their parents, "I'm gay." The deadly monologue goes something like this:

1. I must have been born this way.
2. If I was born this way, God made me this way.
3. If God made me this way, how can there be anything wrong with it?
4. It is my nature and I must be true to my nature.
5. If it's my nature, I can't change.
6. If I try to change, I would be trying to go against my nature, and that would be harmful.
7. Accepting myself as gay feels good – I feel like a thousand pound load has been lifted off my back – so it must be okay.
8. If people can't accept my being gay, something is wrong with them.
9. If people don't accept my being gay, then they don't accept <u>me</u>, because that is who I am.

These nine statements are all false because they are all based on the acceptance of the <u>homosexual identity</u> as a statement of truth. Daughter says, "Mom and Dad, I'm a lesbian." Dad asks, "What makes you think you are a lesbian?" The daughter responds, "Because I'm sexually and emotionally attracted to women and not to men." Mom then asks, "Why do you think you are sexually and emotionally attracted to women?" The daughter replies, "Because I'm a lesbian." This is circular reasoning. Such "reasoning" leads to identifying and labeling people as homosexual! The fact that a man is attracted to a man is just that; the fact that a woman is attracted to a woman is just that! It is not an identity.

The Gay Liberationists declare a <u>homosexual identity</u> on every occasion of any homoerotic impulse. It is part of their agenda and it is a lie! The formation of sexual identity is far more complicated than they would have us believe. Is Michael, who is now the biological Father of two children and who passionately loves his wife, a homosexual because he still has some homoerotic thoughts and impulses? Absolutely not! Should Michael divorce his wife and run back to the gay community? Absolutely not.

Michael as a married man still contends to this day with homoerotic thoughts and fantasies. Yet he lives within a Spirit empowered identity. He walks in substantial but not complete redemption. Every day he grapples with the not-yet of the rule of God. But Michael's experience of an incomplete and imperfect redemption is mine as well. I entertain hetero-erotic thoughts and struggles that challenge my marital covenant. Should I abandon my marriage of 40 years because I struggle with lusting after women other than my wife? No! A thousand times no! Do my struggles invalidate my identity in Christ? Absolutely not!

The formation of a gender identity can be a very fragile as well as dynamic process. Beverly has had babies with two men to whom she sold her body for drugs. She attends AA meetings in which men typically try to hit on her every week. She has seldom felt love from men, including her Father. She now wonders why she is emotionally drawn to women! Men represent a war zone for Beverly. Women represent safety. The Gay Liberationist declare, "Beverly is a lesbian!" The fact is Beverly is confused, alienated and drug infested. Beverly doesn't have an *identity*, much less a lesbian identity!

The stories are legion. <u>Don't label</u>! Listen to the stories. Every story is different. The Lord is redeeming all our stories. But the fundamental redemption is not sexual. It is <u>human</u>. "You are a beloved child of God." This happens within a community that does not "hit on" Beverly, but loves on Beverly. This redemption by the Triune God within a real family of Mothers, Fathers, sisters and brothers begins the healing of our gender identities.

DISCUSSION QUESTIONS

1. Discuss the healing presence of Christ and the hiding of the same-sex struggler.
2. Discuss self-acceptance and where it comes from.
3. When does unforgiveness become a bigger issue than the sin already in need of forgiving in your life? Discuss.
4. Discuss the healing of memories as the deepest form of forgiveness.
5. Do you agree with C.S. Lewis' description of the diabolical and the animal?
6. Why is forgiveness at the heart of our healing?
7. Discuss the labeling of homosexuality as an identity. Have you labeled? Why is it inaccurate and dangerous?
8. Discuss the sexual identity issues of Michael and Beverly.

All of Us Get Healed Together or Nobody Gets Healed: Marriage, Chaos, Love Disorders, Sexual Inversions and Gender Confusions

෴

"We no longer believe in the sanctity of marriage." So said Joseph McNight, SMU family law professor and one of the architects of the Texas Family Law Code. He was referring not only to the no-fault divorce laws in Texas, but also to the attitudes and values of the dominant culture in Texas. The divorce rate in Texas, outside or inside the Church, runs about the same as the wider culture. We certainly believe in getting married but we don't believe in the "High Holiness" of marriage. We practice a serial monogamy. We create our vows, discarding "till death do us part." We shape marriage and divorce to suit our purposes rather than allowing the Lord to shape us for His purposes through marriage.

The debacle of divorce in America gives an opening to the Gay lobby. If marriage is not what it used to be for heterosexuals, then marriage can become what is needs to be for homosexuals. Marriage can be <u>redesigned</u> to be what it needs to be for all of us, heterosexual and homosexual alike. How can we effectively minister to same-sex strugglers if we aren't discipling the Church into Jesus' teachings on marriage, love, sex and true masculinity/femininity? The issues raised by the Gay Liberationists regarding marriage and love cannot be effectively answered until we believe and more effectively embody what the New Testament says about marriage and love.

The Church, as she ministers to all of her members – including her same-sex strugglers, must be clear in her teaching regarding the nature of marriage. What Churches embody regarding marriage speaks louder than what we actually articulate with our mouths. Unfortunately, as a family law practitioner in the Texas "Bible Belt" I have found that the sanctity of marriage is not honored either within the Church or outside of it. The grave condition of marriage in the Church should not cause us to give up on marriage. It should cause us to confess our sin and pray for "renewed minds" regarding marriage.

MARRIAGE – WHAT IS IT?

Three views of marriage now compete for our allegiance: the covenant model, the choice model and the commitment model.

The first view is the covenant man-woman model as articulated in Genesis 1 and 2, Ephesians 5:25ff, Mark 10:1-9 and Matthew 19:1-9. It is based on the foundation of three beliefs or assumptions: (1) Marriage is a unique covenantal community based on the differences and union of the sexes. (2) Marriage is also a social institution that links prior and future generations through the conception, birthing, rearing and sending out of children. (3) Marriage is a legal status that is designed to preserve, protect and promote this institution, especially for the benefit of children, parents and grandparents. Constitutionally, in the U.S.A. we have traditionally guaranteed the right of every American to enter into that legal status.[28]

The choice model has competed with the covenant model since the advent of the 1960's sexual revolution in America. It has four basic beliefs/assumptions: (1) Individuals should be free to choose their sexual partner from either sex. (2) Traditional marriage, as an institution that embodies certain views of sexuality, morality and

---

[28] David Argon Coolidge "The Questions of Marriage" in Homosexuality and American Public Life, Christopher Wolfe (ed.), (Dallas, Spencer Publishing Company, 1999), page 212.

family, is no longer the norm. (3) The law should leave individuals free to contractually create their own domestic relationships. (4) Constitutional law in America should enforce individual rights to freely "contract relationships" over and against legislative attempts to restrict the range of options to traditional marriage.

The commitment model being adopted by an ever-increasing number of Americans constitutes a middle way between covenant and choice, but it must not be confused with the covenant model. The following are the basic beliefs and assumptions behind the commitment model: (1) Every individual seeks intimate relationships. Sex is a way of expressing intimacy. (2) Intimacy grows best within a framework of seasonal commitment, not lifetime covenanting and such commitment is not necessarily between a man and a woman. (3) Couples, children and society benefit from committed rather than promiscuous relationships, whether they are heterosexual or homosexual relationships. (4) It is reasonable, therefore, for the law to encourage committed relationships. (5) Marriage is the central legal institution of commitment in American society. Therefore, marriage or something equivalent to it should be open to every couple, homosexual and heterosexual alike.

In the Church, a hodgepodge of all three models now exists. In fact, elements of the choice model and/or the commitment models now dominate the body life of most Evangelical churches! The Texas No-fault divorce laws reflect the dominance of choice and commitment over covenant. The Church for the most part has quietly given up on the notion of covenant. The gay lobby, at this time, is arguing that given the erosion of the <u>covenant</u> dimension of the traditional model, it makes no sense to hang on to the <u>couple</u> (male-female) dimension of the model. Therefore, their argument concludes that it now makes no sense to outlaw homosexual marriage. I argue that given the erosion of the covenant model, it is time to redouble our teaching and repent of our failure to empower one-another to live out our marriage covenants.

Today's Church, often in captivity to the world, is not even aware of the two models of marriage that have stolen their way into the heart of the Church. The Church must be discipled into the Biblical reality of marriage. Then her witness to the Kingdom of God within her marriages will call her same-sex strugglers on to a more mature life.

The moral failure of the Church regarding divorce includes the adoption of the world's <u>values</u>, thus making divorce inevitable. We value happiness and fulfillment above all else. It is necessary that we demonstrate to those caught in the grips of homosexuality and all other forms of relational futility the goodness and beauty of the sexual life expressed as God intended it to be – within the bonds of marriage. To a great extent we have failed. We need not try to excuse ourselves. It's time to confess that we no longer value <u>covenant</u> love as taught in our Scriptures, repent and go on with a good deal more humility. The path (covenant marriage) is still the right path, though the Christian pilgrim frequently does not walk it! Instead, we choose worldly values that make covenant unfaithfulness inevitable!

It's tough to toe the line on homosexual marriage when we have already blurred the lines of distinction between good and evil in the Church! Our Church culture has unwittingly followed the lead of psychologist Carl Jung and others in blurring the distinction between good and evil. We did it by disregarding what Jesus said regarding marriage, divorce and remarriage (Mark 10:1-10; Matthew 19:1-9). We allow people to get divorces, leave churches, relocate and reinvent themselves and then go back to church as if <u>nothing has happened</u>. Evil becomes a "fresh new start." We dare anyone to cry out, "This makes no sense! What about Jesus?"

In the traditional Church prior to the mid 60s adults assumed the burden and accepted the blows of life so their children could grow and develop in peace. Today, in the Church, it is children who bear the burdens while parents seek their own <u>pleasure</u>! This is IN THE CHURCH! Why do we do this?

We moved from understanding that life is a training ground for the New Heaven and New Earth to believing that this life is a place to experience all the happiness possible before we die. We are dead wrong! All of this calls us to repent in order to have any credibility when trying to address the issue of homosexual marriage.

THE INVERSION OF SEX

Now sex in America is understood as an inversion upon the self, whereby my eyes turn in their sockets to look at "me, me, me" all the time. Personal pleasure, <u>self</u>-fulfillment and worst of all, freedom from social responsibility are the primary standards of expression. This revolution of the eyeballs inward detaches us from our "lovers" and the children such "loving" produces. I am surprised at how many men, 19 years to 60 years of age, can and do walk away from the children they fathered. There are "Christian men" who living this inverted, small-minded life, have no or very little passion for their own offspring. As a family lawyer, I can tell you that if the judges would allow it, millions of divorced men and those who never married the mothers of their children would execute affidavits terminating their parental rights tomorrow. Sex just for "me, me, me" turns hostile toward the lover when she doesn't satisfy my wants. Refusal to even pay for child support is typically a way of getting at a lover who angers me with her rejection. The inversion of sex for personal pleasure leads to unwanted and unaffirmed children!

It takes instruction in Biblical marriage and a measure of maturity to understand and know in our hearts that sexual intercourse is for the purpose of embodying and deepening the one-flesh marriage of a man and woman (Genesis 1, 2), before it is for the purpose of procreation and before it is for the purpose of pleasure (Song of Solomon). It is not a private act intended for the solitary pleasure of a participant. It <u>serves</u> the marital union-oneness-togetherness. It takes some spiritual maturity to have healthy union-enhancing sex! It comes as we grow up, as we mature in the Spirit.

If sex is primarily for pleasure then why can one man get a divorce because sex with his first wife was not as good as sex with his girlfriend and yet another man cannot get a divorce from his first wife because sex with his first wife was not as good as sex with his new <u>boyfriend</u>? It makes no sense to the gay community or me. If pleasure is <u>king</u> then the license given to heterosexuals must be given to homosexuals.

This sexual inversion is in the Church. It is one reason we have difficulty ministering to the same-sex struggler. We find ourselves on as slippery a slope as they are. As we hear them describe their desires we have to face our own desires, and it is troubling. After all, if our eyes scout a more pleasurable lover shouldn't we pursue it? And if that's true for me then how can I minister the nature of Biblical sexuality into a same-sex struggler?

DISORDERED LOVE

"We love confusedly in fallenness. The journey of life is for setting love in order."[29] Some homosexuality has to do with unmet same-sex love needs that have been eroticized. We are starved for *storge* (family love), but instead of entering into the family of God and developing love relationships with Fathers, Mothers, sisters and brothers, we make up the deficit with eroticized sexual encounters. This is a part of the confusion of sin. We will not find the family love we need in a one-night stand. Love, highly eroticized "love", is now the dominant "love" of our media culture. This eroticism is little more than a sexual encounter. It is a fast available means of anesthetizing the pain of loneliness and depression and feeding our lust. Dangerous anal sex with a stranger does not feed our longing for family. It perpetuates the love disorder!

If I as a child did not receive lots of agape – God's need meeting love for all of us – or philia – friendship love – or *storge* - family love – then I am lonely for love. I am very needy of being loved as I am also in need of loving – of caring for others real needs. But, if I am unaffirmed and love-starved what I desire most terrifies me!

Therefore, terrified of loving relationships of risk, service and friendship, I am seduced by the media's description of love: erotic orgasm. It will be my moment of love. It appeals to our lustful side, but its lack of continuity or commitment appeals to us as well. Therefore, I go for erotic "love" which turns out to be just sexual orgasm. The fact is I am scared of love; I do not think it can happen for me and so I settle for sex, only to be left lonely again. And so the

---

[29] Mario Bergner <u>Setting Love in Order</u> (Grand Rapids, Baker Books, 1995), p.70.

cycle continues; lonely, scared of agape love, I battle the temptation but finally I settle for a sexual release when love is what I hunger for. This is a love and relational disorder. It also becomes an addiction. It becomes the way of medicating my pain – my loneliness – my depression. I hear this story too often in the Church where I pastor![30]

We must live in Gardens of Love – places where agape, philia and *storge* flourish. Places where we receive the delight of God's love in prayer, faith and relationships. Otherwise we battle a perverted Eros all alone.

Eros is not a demon. Eros, classically understood, is our longing for completion in love. God made us to long for soul mates, sexual partners with whom we may live our lives. When Eve was created Adam shouted "At last, bone of my bone and flesh of my flesh." The Creator God was meeting Adam's longing for completion. The Song of Solomon celebrates the erotic longing of loved ones for the full completion of marital love – friendship, sexual passion, commitment and celebration of the body. It's all there. Eros is not sex! Eros pursued as just sex leads to dangerous sexual encounters with strangers! Eros defined as sex alone is a love disorder that must be marked as a lie! We must teach the great loves and disciple one-another in walking out their meanings!

The disordering of love within us is often connected with our own failure to receive the grace of God. Reception of God's love for me provides significance and security for me. As I receive God's love I begin to be able to love myself as God loves me. Whoever does not love himself or herself is an egotist! That is they are continually focused on themselves; "It's always about me." They are an egotist because they are never sure of their identity and are always trying to find themselves. That's one reason the Apostle Paul in his letters to churches was continually affirming the new identities of

---

[30] Mario Bergner's book Setting Love in Order (Grand Rapids, Baker Books, 1995), especially chapters 3 and 4, is a wonderful discussion of the love disorder issues in our lives. The book also describes the way out of the wasteland of disordered love.

these new churches as the beloved of God, children of God, and saints of the most High God![31]

It is as new creations that we know a new identity as beloved children of God. This new identity is affirmed again and again by the Body of Christ. It is from within a community of friendship and family where God's unconditional love lives in us, liberating us from the disorders of unredeemed eros that we learn to live the great loves! Let's find a place and make the time to sit, talk and pray the truth regarding the great loves of our lives into one-another!

ROMANTIC LOVE DISORDER

We live to teach and embody the love of God. All of us <u>need</u> to be loved and to love. No doubt about it, in our world sexual and romantic love are everything, leading to rampant love disorders within our marriages. For example, Paul in Ephesians 5 tells husbands to "love your wives as Christ loved the Church." In other words, we are to love because we are married. We aren't married because we love. The preacher asks the groom, "Will you love her" not "Do you love her?" The wedding question, "Do you promise to love her?" is always answered, "I do!"

But does the average bride and groom understand the significance of the vows? The vows of love – covenantal vows – provide the love foundation for the marriage. Covenant love itself is based on the solid rock of the Lord Jesus Christ! However, up until the moment the preacher asked the wedding question the groom as well as the bride were basing much if not everything on romantic-sexual sparks between them. The preacher's question constitutes a <u>momentary</u>, highly ritualized deviation from the romance-erotic world. Neither the bride nor the groom understands the significance of the vow question! The bride and the groom are not <u>grounded</u> in their Christian vows!

That's why three years later the groom can say to me "I don't love her anymore." It is the disordering of love. The groom means, "I don't feel the feelings I should feel and I have a right to feel in

---

[31] 1 Corinthians 1:1-3

order to be married." The groom doesn't understand that now is the time to hear Paul's words, "Husbands love (agape) your wives as Christ loved the Church." And so he calls a family lawyer. He thinks love is primarily a feeling that <u>happens</u> to him, rather than a covenant made to join God in loving his wife.

The failure to love as Christ loves will kill all romance and sexual desire for one another. When we emotionally neglect or beat up one another our feelings die. It is God's love in us that nourishes sexual attraction. Good friendship nurtures good lovemaking.

The redemption of our loves within the Body of Christ will bless all of us, including same-sex strugglers who also need to learn the dimensions of love. Within the Church we live to TEACH AND MODEL THE ORDERING OF LOVE. It is in these relationships in the new Family of God that we learn to Order Love! We begin to <u>see</u> how crucial agape (God's unconditional, need meeting love) is, how we long for *storge* –family love, how precious true philia (friendship love) is, and how wonderful <u>true</u> eros (our longing for completion) is. We begin discerning the love distortions and the love disorders within our fallen world! Heterosexual and homosexual alike are in great need of the orderings and feedings of love as administered by the Holy Spirit of the Triune God!

RECOVERY OF MASCULINITY

The statistics indicate that sexual identities are profoundly shaped by the immediate culture around us in childhood and adulthood. Yet it is not true that our sexual identities are unalterably engraved in stone by age 6 or 7. The reality for many people is much more dynamic than that!

Powerful redemptive relationships with same and opposite sex brothers and sisters in the Body of Christ teach us the meaning of true masculinity and true femininity that we missed in our families. The notion that because I am not Arnold Schwarzneggar I am not masculine is a lie. We have a masculinity defined by whether we were jocks! We have a femininity defined by pictures of cosmetically made-up women. Nobody looks like those women, including those women!

For many adults estrangement from their Fathers goes back to early childhood. At puberty and adolescence these children were listening for a Father's masculine voice they never heard. It is the strong masculine love and affirmation coming through that voice that convinces us that we are truly, finally and appropriately separate from our Mothers. We were born not knowing ourselves as separate from our Mothers. We then begin the arduous task of separating our identity from hers. The <u>crisis of sexual identity</u> consists in the fact that this separation and affirmation has not happened for many adult men and women. Frequently, we do not come out of puberty and adolescence affirmed as persons.[32] Therefore, we have legions of unaffirmed men and women suffering from a great deal of gender confusion. That is, they know they are male or female. What they don't know is "Am I a real man or real woman?" What is a real man or real woman?

It is crucial at this point to point out that "gender confusion" is not homosexuality. A male is "gender confused" who has numerous sexual encounters with women while running from emotional intimacy and relational accountability with women. Joe, an unaffirmed young man of 35, was alienated and terrorized by his Father's temper. His manliness was never affirmed because of the great emotional distance between him and his Father. Joe did not sense his own masculine strengths, his own ability to do the things a real husband and Father does. Such challenges created tremendous anxiety in him. His anxiety was sinfully channeled into a series of sexual relationships with women, looking for affirmation from women in sexual intercourse. But the needed affirmation could not and did not happen.

Joe finally began to see his need to move past the sins of emotional immaturity into a mature masculine identity. He saw the attractions of marriage, but was terrified of it. Joe benefited from professional counseling. But he also benefited from the Fatherly and brotherly affirmations of his masculinity - a masculinity he did not recognize. He already had much strength, including vocational accountability and financial responsibility, which he had not recognized as <u>signifi-</u>

---

[32] Leanne Payne, <u>The Crisis in Masculinity</u>, (Grand Rapids, Baker Books, 1995), page 25.

cant masculine qualities, equipping him for marriage. The Church at this point became the Father he missed through adolescence. It's not too late. He had no idea how strong he was! The Church's prayers and affirmations in a real live Body is healing him, knitting back together those parts of him that have been split off from him. He is beginning to recognize his strengths as a man. Joe's story is about "gender confusion," but it is not about homosexuality.

Unaffirmed men also include the typical angry male prone to love macho violence. This unaffirmed man, threatened by emotional intimacy with women and scared of same-sex strugglers, has no idea what place gentleness or tears have in the masculine identity. This "man's man" gender confusion also has nothing to do with homosexuality.

Often what homosexual lovers admire in other men will be their own unaffirmed characteristics, those from which they are separated, cannot see and therefore cannot accept as part of their own being. Those attributes are projected onto another person. Leeanne Payne says that homosexual activity is often merely the <u>twisted</u> way a person takes into himself in the mistaken way of a cannibal those attributes of his own personality from which he is <u>estranged</u>! He consumes these desired masculine characteristics in a homosexual relationship with a man who has these characteristics. The Church exists to affirm the masculinity of this unaffirmed man, thereby making the cannibal relationship an obvious waste of time.

The Church functioning as a Spiritual Father to a same-sex struggler affirms a rich masculinity, not a "jock" masculinity defined by society – not baseball, basketball, and football but the good, the beautiful and the true, the entire range of masculinity. We sit and listen and tell our stories, then we affirm the masculinity of one who has been separated from his masculinity from childhood. We identify the truth, the strengths and masculinity our dear brothers have never seen in themselves. We pray listening prayers over our dear brother or sister that by the power of the risen Christ they might see with new illuminated eyes who they are as a real man or a real woman!

The rediscovery of true masculinity and femininity is an ongoing work of the redemptive work of Christ in the Church. Sin has confused us as to who we are. Cultural factors dominate us. For example, we act as if we are constitutionally constructed so as to almost never cry. The fact is we don't cry more because we are immigrants from Northern Europe instead of Southern Europe! Real men cry in Italy and Sicily. Real men cry in Israel. Jesus <u>wept</u> on several occasions! Real men manifest the full range of emotions! Any other notion constitutes significant gender confusion!

What we have often thought of as feminine is a part of the masculine psyche. A man without gentleness, kindness and an eye for beauty for all of God's creation, not just for women, is a carica-ture of a man. What some people call a "man's man" is a <u>freak</u> – an underdeveloped, misguided male! C.S. Lewis reminds us that all of us are feminine <u>responders</u> to God. All of us must receive the word (sperm) of God into our souls. "What is above and beyond all things is so masculine that we are all feminine in relation to it."[33]
The ministry of redeeming our masculinity and femininity must be going on among <u>all of the member of Christ</u>'s body all of the time. The redemption of same-sex strugglers will be only a small part of this great work of God!

DISCUSSION QUESTIONS

1. Which of the three marriage models do you ascribe to and why?
2. What model of marriage is being embodied in the church where you now belong?
3. What is the primary purpose of sexual intercourse? Discuss in light of the notion of the inversion of sex.
4. Identify the loves in your life and any love disorders.
5. Which loves hold your marriage together? Prioritize.
6. Distinguish between sex and gender issues.
7. What is masculinity and what is femininity?
8. Discuss the Church's ministry to the unaffirmed males and females in the Church.

---

[33] <u>Ibid.</u>, page 72. Leeanne Payne quotes from C.S. Lewis though not giving the precise cite in her notes.

The Last Forty Years

❧

"When it comes to sex, isn't the Church taking positions that are just out of step with what's cool?"

"How can the Church oppose homosexual marriages, divorce, premarital sex and abortion? The Church is way out of step with today's progressive society."

These comments assume the Church must eat the fruit of the sexual revolution. The last forty years have clearly seen a "sexual revolution" in the United States. Compare, for example, Hollywood's handling of human sexuality in the movies made before and after the 1966 release of *The Graduate*. Our society, sexually speaking, can best be described as a sexual wilderness on it's way to becoming a sexual disaster area. Freedom from restraint, commitment, virginity, and commandments has not ushered in the bliss expected in the 1960s. Lets look at what has happened over the last forty years to change the way we live our lives!

Within the last forty years the following significant events have occurred, creating a new climate of sexual morality directly impacting on the issue of homosexuality:

Medical and Scientific Inroads

The technology of the pill and penicillin in the 1960s and their subsequent refinements offered us sex without disease, sex without pregnancy and most importantly, sex without accountability. In 1968 the new sex technology seemed to offer us the Promised Land.

In 2006 it looks more like the aftermath of a nuclear war zone. Our technology far exceeds our accountability, morality and conscience. Though we have the pill and penicillin and much more science at our disposal we secure 1 million abortions a year and live with an epidemic of sexually transmitted diseases, including but not limited to AIDS. Technology has helped invert sex into the never-ending inquiry, "Am I happy yet?" Within this moral chaos the homosexual lobby has made enormous inroads.

Removal of Homosexuality from the APA Diagnostic and Statistical Manual

In 1973 the American Psychiatric Association made the decision after an intense lobbying by Gay Rights activists to no longer consider homosexuality a psychological illness. Since 1973 and in response to an ongoing attempt by gay activists within the APA to make it a violation of professional ethics to treat homosexuality, even when the patients wish it, a number of professionals formed an organization called NARTH – the National Association for Research and Treatment of Homosexuality. NARTH has grown to more than four hundred members.

One of the founders of NARTH, Charles Socarides, M.D., a member of the American Psychiatric Association and a clinical professor of psychiatry at the Albert Einstein College of Medicine in New York, has been involved in a heated exchange of letters with Richard Isay, M.D., a homosexual activists and psychoanalyst and longtime member of the APA on the subject of homosexual change. Isay contends that "helping" a homosexual to change is abusive. Socarides responds arguing that if there is an abuse it is in the use of psychiatry to advise patients and their families to "relax and enjoy homosexuality; you're only neurotic if you complain."[34]

Robert Spitzer, a New York psychiatrist and a man making no profession of faith nor having any membership within any church, began in 2000 to clinically study the change in sexual orientation claims of members of the ex-gay movement. In 1973 Spitzer had voted to remove homosexuality from the APA Diagnostic and

---

[34] Jeffrey Satinover, Homosexuality and the Politics of Truth (Grand Rapids, Michigan, Baker Books, 1996), pg. 183.

Statistical Manual. The findings of his 2000 study were the subject of a paper he read at the APA's meeting in May of 2001. Spitzer's paper concluded that some gay men and lesbian women have changed their sexual orientations. His conclusions undermined a fundamental tenet of the Gay-Rights movement: the immutability of sexual orientation. Spitzer's research sparked a spate of articles and books both critiquing and defending his research methods and conclusions.

The Ex-Gay Movement

Since May of 2001 the best researched, most helpful and best balanced study of the "ex-gay" literature and the organizations involved on both sides of the issues is Tanya Erzan's 2006 book Straight to Jesus (Sexual and Christian Conversions in the Ex-Gay Movement published by University of California Press. Erzan, a research oriented social scientist who is now assistant professor of Comparative Studies at Ohio State University, does not agree with the agenda of the Christian ex-gay movement but neither does she agree with the Gay Liberation dogma of genetic immutability.

Though Erzan criticizes as too limiting the Christian Right's absolute definition of homosexuality as a threat to marriage, a developmental condition or a sin to be overcome, her research leads her to conclude "the lives of ex-gay men and women demonstrate that sexual and religious identities are never static or permanent."[35] Erzan is clearly acknowledging real change in the sexual and religious identities of many of those she studied.

She has also interviewed many who either failed to change or never desired to change. Being an advocate of religious and moral pluralism, Erzan argues in conclusion for more inclusive ways of including within our communities practices, identities and arrangements now considered irreconcilable by the opposing parties. She is looking for middle ground which would allow for ex-gay organizations and at least Civil Unions in every state for gay and lesbian couples.

---

[35] Tanya Erzan, Straight to Jesus, (Berkeley, California, University of California Press, 2006), p. 230.

It is significant that Spitzer and Erzan, after hundreds of interviews and a great deal of research of ex-gays and ex-gay organizations, concluded that real changes from homosexual to heterosexual orientations had occurred in many of those whom they studied.

Eisenstadt v. Baird

In 1972 Eisenstadt v. Baird, a U.S. Supreme Court case, struck down a Massachusetts law that prohibited the prescription or sale of contraceptives to unmarried people. Rather than tying privacy in reproductive decision making to marital intimacy the Eisenstadt decision opened up the right to married or single, both free from unwarranted governmental intrusion into decisions to bear or conceive a child outside wedlock. This decision is one of many decisions exalting the portable individual rights of privacy above the institutions of marriage, family, church or government. The unrestrained notions of privacy and consent erode the public-institutional understanding of marriage, making it a private optional choice with little public significance. Cases such as Eisenstadt might be justified on the grounds of the impossibility of enforcing such private behavior, but the legal reasoning clearly functions to weaken marriage.[36]

Roe v. Wade

During this forty year window Roe v. Wade (1973) opened the door to legal abortion, which resulted in a multiplication of abortions, climbing to at least one million a year over the last twenty-five years. According to ethicist Peter Singer of Princeton University, "The sanctity of human life ethic is a mere relic of outmoded religion."[37] Professor Singer in defending abortion does not try to hide the fact that it is killing, indeed the killing of a human being.[38] The abortion issue signifies that we are now in a post-Christian era.

---

[36] Don Browning and Elizabeth Marguardt, "Liberal Cautions on Same-Sex Marriage," The Meaning of Marriage, Robert P. George and Jean Bethke Elshtain, eds. (Dallas, Texas, Spence Publishing Comp., 2006), p. 33.

[37] Peter Singer, Practical Ethics (Cambridge, Cambridge University Press, 1979), Chapters 4 and 6.

[38] Ibid., chapter 6.

In Roe v. Wade the Supreme Court ruled that state action regarding abortion was unconstitutional in the first trimester of pregnancy, permissible after the first trimester in order to protect the health of the mother, and permissible in order to protect potential life only at viability (about 24 weeks), prior to which time the state's interest in fetal life was deemed not compelling. This rather careless and arbitrary placement of boundaries is already something of an embarrassment, thanks to growing knowledge about fetal development and especially sophisticated procedures for performing surgery on the intrauterine fetus, even in the second trimester. In other words, a pregnant woman who wants a little girl can submit herself to a sonogram weeks before viability, find out she's having a boy and abort her child – no questions asked. It's about the mother's rights! The homosexuality debate is now occurring in the wake of the abortion debate and is framed by similar issues. In both instances it is no longer about right or wrong. It is about rights.

Nature or Nurture: Born Gay

Scientific studies popularized in the 1980s and 1990s suggested that there is a biological causation to homosexuality. Parents Magazine ran an article by two Florida Atlantic University researchers debunking parental influence and championing biological conditions. The original conclusions from these studies as trumpeted in the press, which will be discussed later, were mistaken. The researchers themselves published subsequent articles denying that biological causation had been or would ever be proved![39] In 1981 the Alfred Kinsey Institute for Sex Research conducted flawed and since discounted research that suggests that homosexuality is inborn, possibly as a result of prenatal hormonal influences. Kinsey

---

[39] It is important that one go beyond the "Gay Gene" sound bites. The Stanton Jones and Mark Yarhouse book Homosexuality The use of Scientific Research in the Church's Moral Debate. Downers Grove, Illinois., Intervarsity Press, 2000) is full of references to the scientific literature. As is Thomas Schmidt's excellent book, Straight and Narrow? (Downers Grove, Illinois, Intervarsity Press, 1995).

is understood to say that 10% of American males are homosexual. This number has also been discounted and revised downward.[40]

Quality of Life Research

During the last twenty-five years some "brute" facts as to the quality of life of those regularly engaging in homosexual sex acts have become public knowledge. They include: (a) a significantly decreased likelihood of establishing or preserving a successful marriage, (b) a twenty-five to thirty year decrease in life expectancy, (c) chronic, potentially fatal liver disease; infectious hepatitis, which increases the risk of liver cancer, (d) a much higher incidence of fatal immune disease, (e) frequently fatal rectal cancer, and (f) a much higher than usual incidence of suicide.[41]

Rights to Privacy and Personal Freedoms

An individual's right to privacy has strengthen and widened in the courts and in society. This right to privacy perpetuates the myth that what I do inside my house is not only no one's business but it has no impact on anyone else's life. The fact is that everything we do in "private" has a rippling effect on our very public society. We are part of a community, which by definition suggests that each member is impactful upon the whole! We are not just a collection of "islands unto ourselves"!

Tolerating one's sexual license has become a moral imperative over the last forty years. All freely chosen sex is an affirmative good. It now remains to what extent we will take this "freedom". Will it include bestiality, pedophilia and sadomasochism? Suffice it to say that consensual sex acts are now more important than and always outweigh any negative social or familial consequences they may cause.

---

[40] Stanton Jones and Mark Yarhouse, Homosexuality, The Use of Scientific Research in the Church's Moral Debate. (Downers Grove, Illinois, Intervarsity Press, 1995), pp 35-38.

[41] Jeffrey Satinover, op. cit., pgs 80-83.

Lawrence and Garner v. Texas

On Friday, June 27, 2003 the Supreme Court of the United States of America in <u>Lawrence and Garner v. Texas</u> struck down a Texas State law banning private consensual sex between adults of the same sex. This case extended every consenting adult's right to privacy. As recently as 1960 every state had an anti-sodomy law. In 37 states the statutes have been repealed by lawmakers or blocked by state courts. The court's ruling apparently invalidates all the anti-sodomy laws pertaining to consenting adults in the remaining 13 states. Laws governing marriage should be unaffected. It is important to note that the Gallop poll now indicates that 60% of Americans believe homosexual relations between consenting adults should be legal, whereas in 1977 only 33% agreed that homosexual relations between consenting adults should be legal.

Civil Unions and Same Sex Marriage

On December 20, 1999 the Vermont Supreme Court in <u>Baker v. Vermont</u> held that the Vermont marriage statutes unconstitutionally discriminated against same-sex couples who seek to establish a permanent, stable family relationship. In March of 2000 the Vermont legislature passes a law granting gays and lesbians the right to apply for a certificate of a civil union. The couple will have the same rights, privileges, obligations and responsibilities as Vermont gives to married couples. If the civil union is not successful, then the couple can apply for a divorce from a Vermont court, just as a heterosexual couple could do.

On May 17, 2004 Massachusetts became the first state in the U.S.A. to legally permit gay marriage. The law allowing same-sex marriage was the outcome of a November 2003 ruling by the Massachusetts Supreme Court in the <u>Goodridge v. Department of Public Health</u> case that declared the prohibition of gay marriage to be a violation of the State's Constitution. Marriage was defined as primarily a private, intimate exclusive union. The generative purpose of the large majority of married couples was set aside and replaced with the idea of marriage as a sexual and affectionate friendship.

The Goodridge case assumes that the Massachusetts Supreme Court has the right to redefine marriage.[42] The legal reasoning of the case undermines the historic bonding and enduring relationship that occurs between parents and their children. As the no-fault divorce revolution entirely ignored the experience of children so does the Goodridge decision. Dismissing the core relation between kin altruism and marriage constitutes an injustice to children.[43]

The polls early in 2005 reflected a deep split as to the issue of legalizing homosexual marriage. 51% oppose and 49% support the legalization of homosexual marriage.

The New Jersey Supreme Court ruled on October 25, 2006 that denying committed same-sex couples the financial and social benefits and privileges given to their married heterosexual counterparts bears no substantial relationship to a legitimate government purpose. The court holds that under the equal protection guarantee of Article I, Paragraph I of the New Jersey Constitution, committed same-sex couples must be offered on equal terms the same rights and benefits enjoyed by opposite sex couples under the civil marriage statutes. The name given to the statutory scheme that provides full rights and benefits to same-sex couples, whether marriage or some other term, is a matter left to the democratic process.

The court seeks to protect individuals from discrimination based on sexual orientation. It is assumed that given the immutability of sexual orientation homosexual people constitute a discriminated against class. Yet the court refused to hold that same-sex marriage is a fundamental right. Fundamental rights are those deeply rooted in the traditions, history and conscience of the people. Therefore, the decision does not mandate same-sex marriage legislation, but it does mandate, at the least, a civil union statute.

As of June, 2007, in the United States, the Commonwealth of Massachusetts recognizes same-sex marriage, while California, Connecticut, the District of Columbia, Hawaii, Maine, New Jersey and Vermont grant persons in same-sex unions a similar legal status

---

[42] Browning and Marguardt, op. cit., p 43

[43] Ibid., p 43.

to those in a civil marriage by domestic partnership, civil union or reciprocal beneficiary laws.

Nineteen states have constitutional amendments explicitly banning the recognition of same-sex marriage, confining civil marriage to a legal union between a man and a woman. Forty three states have statutes defining marriage as the union of two persons of the opposite sex. A small number of states ban any legal recognition of same-sex unions that would be equivalent to civil marriage.

Numerous lawsuits have been filed in state courts all over the U.S.A. contesting the constitutionality of the state's marriage amendments which define marriage as a union between two persons of the opposite sex.

The New Paganism

Socially, we have made two moral leaps backwards in the last forty years. The first was the leap from the moral commandments of scripture concerning sex to sex that does not <u>harm anyone</u>. The second leap jumped further backwards into the darkness contending that the issue is not whether anyone is harmed, but whether the sex act occurred with <u>mutual</u> consent. The fact that we might abort the life resulting from orgasm or we might get AIDS from anal sex carries no moral weight.

Topping off the new moral climate of the new paganism is the notion of man as a biological machine. Ironically, the notion of "freely chosen sex" is a misnomer within the reigning new paganism. For if man is only a biological machine then he/she has sex not because he/she <u>will</u> but because he/she must. Therefore, gay AIDS victims and heterosexual carriers of STDS are not sinners in need of repentance but martyr-victim-heroes!

Cultural Christianity

The influence of Jesus Christ the Lord has decreased *within the Church* in the U.S.A. Nominal cultural Christianity is replacing passionate relational Christianity. The polls indicate the percentages of people who claim to be Christians has remained high. Yet many of those who claim to be Christian attend church only a few times a year. The influence of Jesus the Lord within their lives has diminished. The morals of the Church are no longer discernibly different from those outside the Church.[44] Attempting to be relevant many churches have become anything but. The local church as an open place for the powerful liberation of homosexuals or for that matter any other sinner is almost nonexistent. The average church is pleasant but not powerful.[45] Most church members have not been empowered or matured into life-changing ministry for the "lepers among us."

The election of a gay bishop within the Episcopal Church of the United States

On June 7, 2003, New Hampshire elected the Reverend Caron Vicki Gene Robinson as the first openly homosexual bishop in the Anglican Communion. This historic action was the culmination of decades of ferment on the issue.

In 1979 the General Council of the Episcopal Church in America affirmed a resolution that said there is no bar in the ordination process to homosexuals whose lives are "wholesome examples." In 1989 Bishop John Shelby Spong ordained Robert Williams, an openly gay and active homosexual, to the priesthood. In 1994 Bishop Spong drafted the Koinonia Statement. This states that homosexuality is morally neutral and supports the ordination of homosexual clergy in faithful sexual relationships.

In February, 1997 the 2nd Anglican Encounter in the South issued the Kuala Lumpur Statement on Human Sexuality that takes the Global North to task for the innovations of ordaining openly homosexual clergy and for blessing same-sex unions that it said "calls into question the authority of the Holy Scriptures." In September of the same year fifty conservative bishops and archbishops from 16 countries released the "Dallas Statement" which affirmed the Kuala Lumpur Statement and declared that Scripture "provides no justification for the Church to ordain non-celibate homosexuals or bless same sex relationships."

---

[44] Ronald Sider, The Scandal of the Evangelical Conscience, (Grand Rapids, Baker Books, 2005)

[45] Larry Crabb, The Safest Place on Earth, (Nashville, Word Publishing, 1999)

In July 23,2003, an assembly of mainstream Anglican bishops, priests and lay people issued a statement from Fairfax, Virginia, stating that the confirmation of Canon Robinson as bishop would "separate the Episcopal Church from historic Christian faith and teaching and alienate it from the fellowship and accountability of the worldwide Anglican family." But on August 5, the House of Bishops of the General Council of the Episcopal Church in America consented to the election of Robinson.

Three observations seem pertinent here: (1) Bishop Spong who has led the move toward ordaining an openly practicing homosexual Bishop no longer acknowledges the validity of the Apostle's Creed. He rejects the notion of Christ's resurrection from the dead, his substitutionary atonement and any notion of Jesus as the incarnate God. (2) The Episcopal diocese in which Spong was bishop has suffered a drastic decline in membership. The Episcopal Church in America is on a quickening numerical decline. (3) The vast majority of those who call themselves Anglicans or Episcopalians now reside outside Europe, the United States or Canada. This would include more than 3 out of every 4 Anglican/Episcopalians in the world. Those third world communions adhere to the historic Christian confession, preach the ancient gospel, oppose the ordination of gay bishops and homosexual marriage, and are presently vibrant growing communities of faith and life. The ordaining of openly gay bishops constitutes a small part of the Episcopal church in America's tragic departure from the vital Spirit empowered confession that Jesus, the incarnate son of God, died in our place for our sins in A.D. 30, was bodily raised from the dead and rules now at the right hand of God.

CONCLUSION

The last forty years has been nothing less than a sexual revolution. The behavior of Americans, the laws, the prevailing notions of right and wrong as to matters pertaining to human sexuality have changed dramatically. The movies, TV and the Internet glorify nudity and the sexual affair, use sex relentlessly and explicitly to sell American products and pump billions of pornographic images into the home computers of the average American house every day. This enormously powerful avalanche of images has blitzed the U.S.A. for forty years. Consenting adults may use their right to privacy to see almost any image of adults behaving sexually. For some reason we draw a line at the point of our children's minority. We prosecute child pornographers. Not because pornography is wrong, but out of respect for children.

The gay agenda is advanced within the entertainment industry, producing movies such as Brokeback Mountain, The Hours and Mulholland Drive and by aggressively using TV to cast homosexuality in a favorable light in shows such as Will and Grace. The power of our technology has far outrun our moral sensibilities.

The fact that within the last forty years fatherlessness has become the number one social problem in America should never go unnoticed by those who seek to understand those factors that contribute to the homosexual identity. The divorce rate of fifty percent or more dramatically impacts on the accessibility of the Father in many instances. Unaffirmed men are legion in both the lily-white churches as well as the minority dominated churches of the U.S.A.

This chapter has dealt with the wider culture in which the debates regarding homosexuality take place. The wider culture has become a dangerous jungle of seductive, well subsidized ideologies. The marketplace is now also full of post-modern spirituality preachers and advocates of new moralities. It reminds historians of Rome at the time of Christ. As did the first and second century followers of Christ let us also out-pray, out-think and out-live the enemies of the Gospel! Let's provide a real church culture of truth and grace, a Garden for those who have been battling same-sex issues in a veritable wasteland.

DISCUSSION QUESTIONS

1. Why haven't Penicillin and the pill removed disease and unwanted pregnancy from the lives of Americans?
2. Do the media's sound bites regarding genetic causation of homosexuality impact on your views of homosexuality?
3. Discuss the declining influence of biblical Christianity in the U.S. Do you see this happening?

4. Discuss the "brute facts of homosexuality."
5. Would changes in the law as to homosexual marriage change your ethical viewpoint?
6. What is pornography and how is it shaping our lives now? Contrast with 50 years ago.

Paganisms – New and Old

A young man reared in the Church says to me, "I still love Jesus but I can't accept what the Church or the scriptures say about sex. I've got to go with what my heart is telling me. I've got to let the real me come out. I'm tired of you body-hating Christians. Every day new discoveries make our positions on sexual morality look increasingly ridiculous." When I hear this song with all it's verses I'm watching a believer move toward something dangerous – something like the sexual Baal worship and child sacrifice of II Kings. When I try to talk about the dangers of the new religion, I get laughed at! The New Paganism is very seductive!

Christianity came into the world of the old paganism. It was commonly thought that people were subject to the determining influences of a multiplicity of gods. No single universal standard of morality was presumed to exist nor generally sought. Individuals were instead driven to worship that which they most craved. Not surprisingly pagan worship was directed towards power, aggression and sexual pleasure.

The idolatry condemned in Hebrew and Christian scripture is not some vague intellectual nodding to a wood or stone model, but rather the repeated attraction to an ecstatic pagan orgiastic form of nature-worship including male and female ritual prostitution in an unlimited variety of sexual forms. In the Old Testament this act of idolatry worshipped Baal and Ashtoreth. In II Kings 23, King Josiah renews the covenant to the Lord. Then he commissions his priests to do away with the Baal worship in the temple and on the High Places around Jerusalem. Josiah also tore down the quarters of the male prostitutes that were in the temple of the Lord. He also stopped the sacrificing of children at the pagan altars! (2 Kings 23:1-11)

In New Testament times idol worship became the worship of female deities, like Aphrodite. The Apostle Paul commanded the Corinthians to stop frequenting the temple prostitutes (1 Cor. 6:12-20). Sex and religion shrines of one form or another have surrounded Israel and the Church since the very beginning. The new paganism of our time is not a skeptical one that disparages all religion, but rather a sex and religion spirit that stands opposed to the one Holy God of Christian and Orthodox Judaism. In other words, the New Paganism is the cultures religion that support many of the ethical positions and legal rulings we oppose.

The appeal of a reemerging paganism stems from the fact that pagan spirituality, like it's predecessors, makes few moral demands on the individual and is more tolerant of individual differences. The admonition is "Follow your bliss."[46] For the new paganism there is no distinction between the will and impulses or between conscious intentionality and unconscious instincts. What's more, the new paganism seeks to make no distinctions. The male homosexual lover who contracts the HIV virus through anal intercourse is considered a hero-martyr because he was acting upon his instincts. Those who act out of their instincts do so not because they may, but because they must. They simply did what they were driven to do. The movie Philadelphia, starring Tom Hanks, makes a hero out of a practicing homosexual who knowingly engaged in dangerous acts of homosexual "love." Although the story deals effectively with ungodly discrimination against Hanks the movie primarily serves to paint Hanks as a heroic man who knowingly subjected himself to great risk.

This understanding of sexual acts emanates from the new paganism's understanding of human motivation, choices and behavior in terms of prior causes. Prior causes determine everything. Therefore, any discussion of morals, meaning, purpose or value is a waste of time. What appears to be a freely acting or choosing agent, man,

---

[46] Joseph Campbell, The Power of Myth (New York, Anchor Books, 1991), p. 285.

is actually a passive entity driven by prior, more elementary influences, such as psychological complexes, structures of the psyche, family influences, earlier experiences, social trends and molecular biology, that is, genes. All areas of seemingly human choices are illusory. Man is no longer a free agent. He is a pre-programmed biomolecular machine. Man as we know him/her has been abolished! It is the fulfillment of C.S. Lewis' prophetic essay, The Abolition of Man.

When we claim to actually see through our choices and motives and behaviors and explain them according to their origins we no longer take our actions seriously. Neither do we take responsibility for our actions. So when we die as a result of our own actions we are not accountable even for our own self-destruction. This also means that the pedophile, the alcoholic or the serial killer are also beyond moral accountability. All of these can point to prior factors that "caused" their behavior. There is no end to the disastrous implications of such reasoning.

Somehow the so-called gay lobby has distinguished homosexuality from almost all other behaviors, arguing that homosexuality captures the real essence of a person's self, leading to the popular attitude that acting on impulses, attractions and desires is essential to personal wholeness and actualization.[47] This is vividly depicted in the 2002 Best Picture nominee, The Hours.

The Hours depicts homosexuality as capturing the real essence of a persons self. The Hours tells the story of the famous lesbian writer Virginia Wolf and two other lesbian women. All three of these women either married or lived with men at one time or another. Julianna Moore's character marries a man, has a son and then decides to abandon her husband and year old son for the lesbian lifestyle. Her son, years later, has sexual relations with men and women, contracts AIDS and dies. One of his mother's last words of reflection on her decision to abandon her now deceased son was simply, "It was worth it."

---

[47] Satinover, Chapter 16, "The Pagan Revolution" pgs 229-248. This discussion of the New Paganism is influenced by Satinover's reflections on the New Paganism as the culture's religion.

Virginia Wolfe is driven to return to London where she can consort with the women of her choice. She declares passionately to her husband in one riveting scene at a train station the necessity of her return to London. Children and husbands must be sacrificed in order to live out the real essence of these women's selves. The movie is dark and dreary with its deadly serious concern that these women be freed up to live out their fantasies, impulse and desires.

At the end of the story Charissa Dalloway, one of the three lesbian women in the play, godlessly reflects on the hopelessness of life in the city at the end of the twentieth century.

> "We live our lives, do whatever we do, and then we sleep – it's as simple and ordinary as that. A few jump out of windows or drown themselves or take pills; more die by accident; and most of us, the vast majority, are slowly devoured by some disease, or, if we're very fortunate, by time itself. There's just this for consolation: an <u>hour</u> here or there when our lives seem, against all odds and expectations, to burst open and give us everything we've ever imagined, though everyone but children (and perhaps even they) know that these hours will inevitably be followed by others, <u>far darker and more difficult</u>."[48]

And so we are left in our dark hours to worship what we crave. Acting on sexual and romantic lesbian impulses becomes the worship of the gods of the body. For that is all there is!

Paganism spiritualizes the instincts. The gods are only projections of our fears and cravings. The new paganism takes what is found in man's human nature as the measure of what is good and makes of it a god. The new paganism, at times, seems polytheistic, the gods being whoever or whatever you say he/she/it is! At other times god seems pantheistic, in that "my body and my spirit are my god." No single moral standard results from the New Paganism. Every man is <u>obligated</u> to do that which is right in his own eyes! In

---

[48] Michael Cunningham <u>The Hours</u>, New York: Fawar, Straus and Girasux, 1998), p. 225.

a world of many alternative spiritualities, there are many alternative forms of ethical living.

Within the new paganism homosexuality appears as a loosely defined aspect of man's multidimensional human sexuality. This view of sexuality can tolerate everything from monogamous sex to bestiality and even sex with children.[49] The Godly standard of sexual behavior is much more narrowly defined than the sexuality of the body gods.

It is important to note that the practice of sex as a god to be worshipped has brought the bitter fruit of a mushrooming abortion culture during the last thirty years. The sexuality of the New Paganism is not friendly towards children. Those who act on impulses have no thought of tomorrow's consequences, much less tomorrow's children. It is also significant to note that the worst human sacrifices in the history of mankind were performed under the <u>humanistic</u> new paganism pretenses of the French Revolution in France, the Communists revolutions of the Bolsheviks in Russia, Mao Tse Tung in China and Nazism in Germany, resulting in the death of over 100 million people.

As the philosophy of the New Paganism advances all remaining behaviors will be accounted for with <u>nothing</u> left to <u>choice</u>! This all-consuming philosophy and technique often inspires resistance, even dread and revulsion, for its end point is appalling: the destruction of the very idea that there is choice, meaning and purpose in human existence. Feminists, minorities and others vigorously resist the idea that their behavior is driven by unchangeable biological factors. For example, black leaders do not buy into the notion that black males are condemned to act in certain ways that reflect the genetics and environment of a prior generation. By contrast, the homosexual community is the only community I know of that does not want to

---

[49] Peter Singer, Professor of Princeton University and author of numerous books including <u>Practical Ethics</u>, argues for ethical consequences as the criteria for judging the merit of all behavior. Singer defends abortion, infanticide, bestiality and even pedophilia, in certain circumstances. See <u>Practical Ethics</u> (Cambridge, Cambridge University Press, 1979), pgs. 106-117, 122-126, 131-156.

find <u>any freedom</u> and choice involved in their way of life and they are <u>fiercely</u> determined to prove that there is no way out![50]

There is a fallacy in the notion that homosexuality is not immoral because of genetics. The claim that homosexuality is genetic is certainly false as a scientific statement. But whether it is true or false is irrelevant. Science cannot distinguish between moral and immoral behaviors based on predetermination. For if we are not <u>predetermined</u> by our genes, then we are predetermined by our families, and if not by our families then by education, and if not by education then by choices, compulsions and addictions.

If free will and choice is a small point within us we are responsible for that small point. We should live our lives as though that point was a <u>gigantic star</u> weightier in magnitude than the weight of all other factors. We wrestle and fight for that point. Deep in our souls we know there is a <u>point</u> of decision-making that can produce an <u>unpredictable</u> outcome! We sense a dignity within ourselves that can <u>rise above</u> the past. Can the man Nelson Mandela, incarcerated for 28 years off the coast of South Africa, be explained by prior causes? What or who lifted him above the brutality of apartheid to love his jailors? Did not Mandela fight the prior causes every day in his jail cell, refusing to be crushed by the injustice and the oppressive isolation?

If we are free at all, it outweighs all the combined effects of prior causes, producing an utterly unpredictable outcome. If we are not free then we are subject to all prior causes and therefore are totally predictable and completely unaccountable! But do any of us live without the notion of freedom and goodness? The freedom and goodness and dignity of man are still points of a turning world.[51]

Much too often our discussions around our actions are replete with recitations of our parents shortcomings and almost nothing else. Those who don't know the past are doomed to repeat it. But those who <u>only</u> know the past are also doomed to repeat the past. There is more to life than prior causes. If I only know the prior causes I will somehow believe that my body is not the agent of my

---

[50] Satinover, op. cit., pgs 122-126.

[51] Satinover <u>Op</u>. <u>cit</u>. p. 129.

choices! I will not acknowledge my own sin and the suffering my sin causes. Rather, I will think of my own mind as the helpless agent of my father's mistakes. Such thinking, if reinforced again and again, locks me into the death of Adam. It is in this thinking "that all die." (Romans 5:12-21)

The man who rages against his children because his Father raged against him throughout his childhood is not just a victim of his Father's anger. Clearly he was victimized; he was sinned against. He has the scars to prove it. But as he lives his life in rage against his own son he clearly acts as a sinner. A sinner is a precious child of God, made in God's image, but who now lives beneath his own dignity, missing the mark, cut off from God and raging against His own son. As this sinner acknowledges his sins to the Father God and receives the amazing forgiveness of God he recovers his own dignity and freedom. He then possesses the grace to forgive his own Father. In other words, some member of this bent family tree has got to straighten up from their victimized identities and courageously declare, "I did it", receive the Lord's grace and then give that grace to those who sinned against them. Then the curse is broken by the grace of Christ. It is in the renewing presence of Christ that all are made alive. (Romans 5:12-21)

COMPETENCE, COMPENSATION, COMPULSION AND COMMUNICATION

Homosexuality as envisioned by the New Paganism of our time is only a small part of the Sexual Disaster. The inadequacy of the alienated New Pagan, his loss of center, power and community can be documented by four terms: competence, compensation, compulsion and communication.

Under competence I refer to the massive knowledge of sexual technique and physiology. It is now assumed that better bodies and better techniques will produce sexual fulfillment. However, sexual technique even in marriage, without a prior and deeper committed intimacy, may produce orgasm but not love-making! The beautiful, sculpted bodies of People Magazine stay married, whenever they marry, for about "ten minutes!" Their weddings often reflect more investment than their marriages!

Many people turn to sex as <u>compensation</u> for their failure to find authentic community and friendship in their cities and neighborhoods. If we can't find love, we can always find sex. If we dare not risk love, we can always risk sex. At this point too much is demanded of the flight to orgasm, a pitiful god idolized by the lonely, the bored and the despairing. Temporary, often dangerous orgasmic flight whether heterosexual or homosexual is a pitiful compensation for the loss of real friendship, stability, loyalty and marital passion.

The <u>compulsion</u> to have sexual relations means that the old commandment "Thou shalt not" has now been replaced by an equally strident "Thou shalt." The Lord God has been replaced by Lord Eros and the dictates of lust. These pressures <u>compel</u> people to make decisions about sexuality that are not according to their free choice. Internal anxiety and guilt have <u>increased</u>, throwing the individual into a sea of relativities and compulsions. This compulsion decreases freedom, increases addiction, increases anxiety and decreases contentment.

The final and perhaps most difficult problem is <u>communication</u> between the sexes. The hope of belonging also contains within it the threat of rejection. Men and women who can neither escape each other sexually nor communicate intimately find themselves destroying one another. It is also common to see a "gay" guy who prefers casual relationships with guys to "serious" love relationships with women. In other words, find the "relationships" that demand the least and stay with them. But doesn't sexual release without continuity and belonging leaves us groaning for liberation from such lonely tyranny?

THE DISASTER DISCERNED

The New Paganism and it's attendant hedonism (pleasure seeking), advocating the gratification of lustful desires without limit, is on the one hand a form of <u>consistent self-centeredness</u>, the purpose of which may be to display power, enhance prestige or experience a little more happiness. But sometimes lustful behavior is not so much an advertisement of the ego's pride as it is a frantic effort to *escape* from the self. The self, finding itself to be inadequate at the center of its existence, seeks escape amidst the various forces, processes and impulses of sex. Random orgiastic sex with a stranger requires far less ego strength than love-making with a covenantal soul-mate!

This escape into lust is now commercialized by pornography. It has become an enormous industry. There are now twice as many hardcore outlets as there are McDonald's restaurants. There are more than 150,000 pornography websites on the Internet, and it is said that the number is growing at the rate of 200 a week. The $14 billion that Americans spend on video pornography is larger than the annual revenue accrued by the NFL, the NBA and Major League Baseball. People pay more money for pornography in America in a year than they do on movie tickets - more than they do on all the performing arts combined.

Pornography exalts sex not intimacy. Pornography promotes sexual idolization, sexual trivialization and sexual violence. Pornography "unleashes our lust" in a world hell bent on self-fulfillment. Pornography is the marriage of two whores: money worship and lust. These two whores, reeking of the demons and the idols, rob us of our humanity. Sex with a perfect virtual reality lover replaces love-making with an imperfect soul-mate. The addiction inherent in this idol dominates our poisoned fantasy life. The guarantee of a solitary orgasm desensitizes us to the reality of real sex with a real loved one. As we pornographers consort with the idols we lose all contact with why we started: we don't know or care to know about our diabolical self-centeredness or our attempt at becoming a beast in order to escape being a man.

Sexual passion by the very power it develops in the spiritual confusion of human sin, serves the same purpose as drunkenness. As drunkenness is a flight into oblivion so are pornography and casual sex flights into orgiastic oblivion. We took the fig leaf off the genitals and put it over the eyes so long ago that we have forgotten the wonder of the eyes as described in the beautiful Song of Solomon:

"You have stolen my heart, my sister, my bride;
You have stolen my heart with one glance of your <u>eyes</u>
With one jewel of your necklace."

Song of Solomon 4:9

We think pornography results from our being too masculine for our own good when in reality it comes from our failure to be masculine with the eyes of a real woman. Pornography is a very passive, addicting behavior that requires no assertion of masculine or Holy Spirit power. The element of sin in pornography is not due to the fact that sex is in <u>any sense</u> sinful. Neither is it due to the fact that "boys must be boys." Pornography results from the fact that "boys didn't know how to be boys and now don't know how to be men." Boys and/or men who are led around by their genitalia are not boys or men. They are masquerading as men!

The New Paganism is impotent in the face of pornography. It has no moral or spiritual discernment. This malaise of pornography, masculine masquerades, lust, etc. which is the work of the idols, must be broken in the church by the Kingdom of God over us, among us and in us. Then there will be liberation from heterosexual as well as homosexual bondage.

ROMANCE ADDICTION

Furthermore, there are still many who are not so addicted to XXX pornography as they are to romance addiction. In a New Age world where Neal Donald Walsh, new age author of the best seller <u>Conversations With God</u>, contends that spiritual authority resides not in the Bible, the pastor, the priest or the Rabbi but in the "highest self" within each of us, we are easily seduced into the flight of romance.[52] The romantic self is generally thought to be the "highest" calling of the self.

Once human relationships are disturbed by man's rebellion against God the vehicle of sin can also be an expression of a <u>despair-boredom</u> that seeks to escape from the self by the <u>deification of</u>

---

[52] Neal Donald Walsh, <u>Conversations With God</u>, New York, G.P.Putnam & Songs, 2005.

another. "You are my destiny." The deification of another is almost a literal description of many romantic statements. "Without you I'd be nothing." "You are my everything." "I'd die without you!" All of these statements are lies! We assign attributes of perfection to partners of "love" beyond the capacities of any human being to bear. This is a love disorder. Usually it has nothing to do with our wives or husbands. It leads to inevitable disillusionment.

Within the void of our hearts we romanticize a lover we cannot have, whether same or opposite sex. We tell ourselves that this myth is worth the whole world. We call this our "higher self" and thus we obey the call, leaving our wives for greater romance with a man or woman. If bored men can romanticize another woman into reality, justifying a divorce, why can't homosexuals romanticize another man, justifying an act of dangerous sexual "bliss?" Both idolatrous romanticizers have lost contact with any spiritual authority and are lost in the noises of modern Baal worship. The worship of the senses feels right and possesses the authority of the gods!

The New Paganism includes the developing New Religious Synthesis, which opposes the worldview of what I term the Revealed Word. It wears a thousand masks.[53] These writers seduce by spinning themselves as at least a blood kin of Biblical Spirituality. They are not. For example, Debbie Ford's book <u>Spiritual Divorce</u>[54] appears at first glance to be a book with a basis in Biblical Spirituality. Titles of chapters include: "Divine Order", "The Path to God", and "Reclaiming Your Divine Light". One of her laws for life is "The Law of Divine Guidance." Tucked away on page 63, Ford tells us who this so-called God is:

"The God I speak of is not an all-powerful presence that lives outside of us, but rather a universal force that lives in the core of our being, connecting us to all that is and all that will be. It's an all-encompassing energy that is both powerful and wise, a force that is often referred to as spirit, love, universal

---

[53] See James A. Herrick, <u>The Making of the New Spirituality</u>, Downers Grove, Illinois, Intervarsity Press, 2003.

[54] Debbie Ford <u>Spiritual Divorce</u> (San Francisco, Harper and Row, 2001).

consciousness, divine order or nature ... God is our knowledge of the truth and that truth is in itself the presence of God."[55]

God is a force, not a Holy Presence, living in the core of our being. God cannot be distinguished from love, order or truth within us. This force, this Highest Self possesses more "spiritual" authority than the Bible, the Koran, or a Rabbi, Priest, or pastor. Neil Donald Walsh, referenced above, wrote a glowing forward to this book. According to Ford and Walsch we must always listen to the dictates of the energy, force, truth, etc. within us as opposed to any <u>spiritual</u> authority outside ourselves.

Ford never refers to good and evil, right or wrong, moral or immoral. We are to just go with the flow of the "Divine Energy" within. She describes in amoral terms falling in love, moving in with her lover and breaking up. She also describes her marriage to Dan and their break-up in non-covenantal, amoral terms. The book has, in places, some good psychological counsel regarding divorce recovery. The problem is that what is essentially a pop-psychology book is pitched as spirituality. It is part of the Alternative Spirituality of our time. It is by post-modern standards a spirituality, but it does not include a personal deity beyond us or a moral order around us.

It is this type of Alternative Spirituality that is exploding among us. It rivals Covenantal Monotheism in the U.S.A. with devotees estimated from 15 to 30 million and growing. If this spirituality can speak of divorce as containing great blessings when it occurs, it will certainly make plenty of room for consensual homosexual love relationships. It simply has no moral categories with which to even discuss many of the issues raised in the homosexuality debate.

John McShane, a family lawyer in Dallas, Texas wrote a preface to <u>Spiritual Divorce</u>. McShane has publicly advocated this Alternative Spirituality in oral and written presentations at the August 2000 Advanced Family Law Seminar of the Texas Bar. At first blush it is a pleasant surprise to hear an attorney publicly encourage other

---

[55] Ibid., p.63.

attorneys to pray with their clients. McShane openly advocates such behavior with the blessing of the Texas Bar.[56]

Given the constitutional limitations imposed on religion in the U.S.A., how can he do this with the obvious approval of the Texas Bar? Because this is spirituality without Church, spirituality without morality, spirituality without a Holy Book, spirituality without a personal transcendent Lord God, spirituality without a creed. It is spirituality as conceived by each person's highest self.

It passes pluralisms tests. The post-modern assumptions regarding the legitimacy of each man's "spirituality" gives it credibility. Those who raise any questions about this being in violation of the First Amendment can be assured that this spirituality is in fact only psychology in spiritual attire. Such toleration will serve to expand the influence of such spirituality. For this spirituality is now allowed a public presence. It is not considered just a private opinion, but a public truth and a necessary part of a good family law practice in a post-modern world.

This brand of spirituality allows for an enormous range of moral and spiritual choices. It is within these alternative pagan spiritualities that homosexual "love" relationships, including marriage, will find increasing acceptance. Even now as I write these words in November of 2006 more than 50% of Americans approve of homosexual marriage. It is not a coincidence that concurrent with these

---

[56] John V. McShane, "Is This All There Is? Specific Strategies for Becoming the New Family Lawyer," <u>Advanced Family Law</u>, Vol. ?, page ?, August 21-24, 2000). McShane's approach does introduce a "spiritual" approach to the practice of family law that improves the culture in which family law is conducted. Clearly he has much to say to his mammon driven, litigiously inclined colleagues that we need to hear. His approach, generally, takes the unnecessary conflict and litigation out of family law. The fact that on the one hand I am warning the reader regarding the New Spiritual Synthesis and its spiritual-moral implications and on the other hand I am pointing out the good that I see in McShane or Ford's approach to life and family law points to the challenge inherent in living among the shadows. It takes constant attentive discernment to neither damn the entire culture nor accommodate ourselves to it. We expect to run into good surprises as well as bad surprises within the wider culture. Advocates of these new spiritualities represent a step away from violent competitiveness. But at the same time, they do not represent the inauguration of the Kingdom of God. They preach "another Gospel."

changes in attitudes toward homosexual marriage during the last twenty years has been the increasing influence of these alternative spiritualities among millions of Americans.

DISCUSSION QUESTIONS

1. Discuss the paganism of biblical times, using scriptural references and any knowledge you may have of these eras.
2. Discuss the new paganism religion that is taking shape around us.
3. What weight do you give prior causes as an explanation of why you behave as you do?
4. What weight do you give free will and the Holy Spirit in explaining why you behave as you do?
5. Where does homosexuality fit within the new paganism view of sexuality?
6. Discuss the similarities and differences between being a victim and a sinful child of God.
7. Discuss the significance of child sacrifice and abortion within the old and new paganism.
8. How does romance as an addiction and philosophy impact our morals?

Nurture, Nature and Our Moral Choices

ᕫᔭᕚᕮ

G ary, a 26-year-old single male, battles with same-sex struggles. As the media give out "Gay-Gene" sound bites Gary asks, "Why fight it, if I'm predetermined to live it anyway?" Gary also wonders why church people speak of homosexuality as just a sinful lifestyle choice when Gary has never had a strong sexual desire for women. Gary is confused by the radical positions of the Gay rights advocates as well as the overly simplistic positions of traditional church people.

It's time to talk about these matters.

Gay rights activists presently advance three disputed propositions: (1) as a matter of biology, homosexuality is an innate, genetically determined aspect of the human body, (2) as a matter of psychology, homosexuality is irreversible, (3) and as a matter of sociology, homosexuality is normal, akin to such other social classes of race and sex.

Traditionalist, often but not always Christians, counter-argue as follows: (1) First, as a matter of biology, homosexuality is not innate, but a choice. (2) Secondly, as a matter of psychology, homosexuality is reversible. (3) Third, as a matter of sociology, homosexuality is not normal, but an illness or a perversion of nature.[57]

---

[57] Jeffrey Satinover, Homosexuality and the Politics of Truth (Grand Rapids, Michigan, Baker Books, 1996), pp. 71-75. The discussion in this chapter is heavily influenced by Satinover's discussion of the causes of homosexuality.

In summary there are now, within today's culture, three big disputed questions: Is homosexuality normal? Is homosexuality the result of nature or nurture? Is homosexuality reversible?

It is my judgment that the best choices regarding understanding homosexual behavior <u>do not</u> hover at the extreme positions of the Gay activists or the uninformed traditionalist. Certainly when the traditionalist argues that homosexuality is only a "perverse lifestyle choice" debunking all other influences, and <u>any</u> scientific evidence in support of biological and/or environmental influences it makes the traditionalist position appear, at best, uninformed and therefore probably untenable.

As a result of recently discovered scientific facts, science <u>has</u> given us an even greater appreciation of innate biology in determining some human characteristics. Therefore, the gay activists prematurely conclude that the Church is involved in the unjust persecution of an innocent minority! The Church's position is now viewed as based on ignorance and prejudice. Furthermore, the argument continues, as a result of scientific and humanistic principles on the one hand and a new age multiplicity of differing cultural standards on the other, the traditional Biblical view is regressively thwarting progress!

It is my judgment that the Biblical position need not be based on ignorance or regressively thwart real progress. Yet the Christian position is not that homosexuality is just a perverse lifestyle <u>choice</u>. Homosexuality may be in part a biological <u>predisposition</u> and/or an environmental conditioning as well as a personal decision. Contemporary Christians should not fear any information science or psychology may provide regarding homosexual behavior. The big headlines, "Genes Cause Homosexuality" of the past decade are gross overstatements of a biological factor in some homosexual behavior. Such headlines are not science! Serious examination of the scientific literature regarding the biology of homosexuality will confirm this.[58]

---

[58] See Jones, Stanton and Yarhouse, Mark <u>Homosexuality – The Use of Scientific Research in the Church's moral Debate</u> (Downers Grove, Ill., Intervarsity Press,

The gay lobby also errs when they argue that recent research can show that the homosexual state is caused entirely by factors beyond the individual's control, especially emphasizing the biological/genetic nature of these "causes." Their conclusion follows that it would be wrong for the Christian Church to condemn homosexual actions or lifestyles! This argument is not based on good science or good moral logic. In the event that science discovered a biological causation factor for pedophilia, murder or alcoholism, this argument would suggest that one could not then make any negative moral judgments regarding <u>any of these behaviors</u>! Such reasoning leads to greater moral chaos!

Science has <u>not</u> eliminated responsibility for sexual behavior. Homosexual persons are not subhuman robots whose acts are predetermined. These people, like all the rest of us, are moral agents who inherit <u>tendencies</u> from biology and environment and who share in shaping their character by the <u>responses</u> they make to their life situation. The question isn't why shouldn't I be able to do what *feels natural* but rather what should I do to bring glory to God?

The narrow questions of homosexuality – what is it, is it normal, is it genetic, is it reversible – have become heated because they point towards the <u>central questions</u> of human nature and morality. How do we understand life and humanness? Is man responsible for his actions? By what authority do we decide between right and wrong? Is it possible for human beings to change? Though biological and/or environmental factors do not give us spiritual or moral answers, it is crucial that disciples of Christ have some knowledge of these factors which impact on our sexual identities from the moment of conception.

GENETICS

Genetic traits are those (like eye color) that are coded by genes.[59] Each gene is a book that provides a complex set of instructions for

2000). Chapter three of this book is a veritable goldmine of information and source references regarding the research into the causes of homosexuality. The authors are meticulous and fair.

[59] Satinover, <u>op. cit.</u>, pp 71-75.

the synthesis of a simple protein. The entire collection of genes that provide codes for a human is vast. Each gene is divided into 23 pairs of chromosomes. Chromosome libraries exist in pairs because each person actually has two instructional genes for every protein, receiving one of every gene from his Mother and another from his Father.

Understanding <u>behavioral</u> traits influenced by genetics becomes more complex. Unlike simple traits, such as eye color, that are programmed by a single gene, most behavioral traits with a genetic background are <u>programmed by multiple genes</u>![60]

Given the necessity of multiple genes to program behavioral traits, the July 15, 1993 National Public Radio report of a new study in science pointing towards a "gay gene" and thus a biological causation for homosexuality, <u>could not</u> be scientifically accurate. In fact, other genetic researchers criticized Dean Hamer, the author of the study, almost immediately and on June 25, 1995 it was confirmed that Hamer was under investigation by the Office of Research Integrity at the Department of Health and Human Services because he may have selectively reported his data. There was no fanfare this time on National Public Radio.[61]

Columbia University researchers Byne and Parsons describe a complex mixture of biological, psychological and social/cultural factors for homosexuality. They conclude that "genetic factors can be conceptualized as <u>indirectly</u> influencing the development of sexual orientation without supposing that they either <u>directly</u> influence or <u>determine</u> sexual orientation per se."[62] We can conclude that a certain genetic constitution may make homosexuality more probable as an option, but it is not the <u>cause</u> of homosexuality. [63]

---

[60]-<u>Ibid.</u>, p. 72.

[61]-<u>Ibid.</u>, pp. 109-113

[62]-<u>Ibid.</u>, p. 93

[63]-<u>Ibid.</u>, p. 93

INNATE

Some traits may be innate, meaning the individual is born with them. An innate trait may be genetic, but it may also be caused by intrauterine influences. These are traits that are influenced by various aspects of the environment of the womb. Hormones, infections, and ingestion of both illicit and prescription drugs influence this environment. There are no studies indicating that innate non-genetic traits cause homosexuality.

FAMILIAL

Other traits may be familial, meaning that they tend to be shared by members of the same family. Family traits may be genetic because they have the same parents and/or innate because the Mother's dietary habits impacted on all her children similarly. Family traits also include environmental traits such as the physical, emotional and moral influences of the family system.

ENVIRONMENT

These influences are not biological, but include the values, standards, peer pressures, habits, laws, ideas and even economic status that weigh in our lives. Jimmy is a good example of how peer pressure combined with false ideas about his identity developed into homosexual behavior. As a young teenager without any strong male influences in his life affirming his masculinity, Jimmy was ridiculed for his high-pitched voice and his sleight build. One day when he was 15 years old he was sexually attacked in a public bathroom by a powerful adult and literally carried away into a gay community where he was told he was gay. Years later when I talked with Jimmy two weeks before he died of AIDS he said to me, "I was never gay." Jimmy was saying he never felt gay. He was always drawn to women. But he believed that because no woman found him attractive he just did what he was supposed to do. Jimmy acted "gay" because of powerful communal pressures that declared his "gayness" and reaffirmed him as a gay man. Jimmy was vulnerable to such pressures at least in part because he was <u>not</u> knitted together with a Body of Christ in which he could have received the Fathering and brothering he missed in his natural family.

DIRECT OR INDIRECT

Direct causes would lead directly to the trait as when genes cause blue eyes. But indirect causes are at work when the tall athletic person chooses to be a basketball player. Choice clearly <u>impacts</u> on the behavior patterns! In fact <u>choice</u> impacts on behavior more than <u>all</u> other influences! For example, a man with homosexual tendencies may have no desire presently to have sex with a woman, but he may choose to live in sexual abstinence, refusing to act out with men, because he <u>chooses</u> to honor the Lord God. At this point whether he is biologically or environmentally predisposed to homosexuality is irrelevant. What if his sister is biologically predisposed to alcoholism? Again, her <u>choice</u> to abstain from all alcohol impacts more on her behavior than all other influences. As with her brother, whether she is biologically or environmentally predisposed to alcoholism is irrelevant.

NON-GENETIC

The <u>non-genetic</u> factors that can influence the development of a behavior pattern fall into four categories:

1.–Intra-uterine (pre-natal) effects such as hormones.
2.–Extrauterine (post-natal) outside the womb physical effects such as trauma, viruses, family interactions, education, the reinforcing effect of the repetition of behaviors.
3.–Choice. Decisions made and then repeated hundreds, even thousands of times. This includes the decision to call one's self a homosexual as well as the decision to act in such a way as to confirm the identity.[64] Choice can become a compulsive pursuit

---

[64]-<u>Ibid.</u>, p. 97

of pleasure, which is in fact our most common human response to distress.

4.–Apart from the genetic factors, psychoanalysts have learned that often in their patients there is an <u>emotional mismatch</u> between the patient and their same-sex parent. Typically the male or female child suffers from a detached same-sex parent.

SUMMARY

Recent studies postulate biologic factors (genetic, hormonal) as the <u>primary</u> basis for sexual orientation. However, there is no evidence at present to substantiate a biologic theory, just as there is no evidence to support any <u>singular</u> psychosocial explanation.[65] Each individual's homosexual behavior is the likely result of a complex mixture of genetic, intrauterine and extrauterine biological factors combined with familial and social factors as well as repeatedly reinforced sinful choices. The role of genetic impulses is probably very small.[66]

These "causes" of homosexual behavior manifest themselves in diverse ways. My conversation with scores of people who are or have behaved as homosexuals reveals an astonishing diversity of sexual dynamics, behavior and attitudes. For example, Gary outfitted his van as a French boudoir and cruised the city most nights. Yet Gary was also very interested in sex with women. But whether it was a man or a woman he wasn't looking for marriage or commitment. Gary was a sexual idolator. John, a married man (to a woman) claimed to have never desired sexual intimacy with a woman. Yet he repressed his homosexuality, made love to his wife only when he was at least slightly intoxicated, fathered two children, and lived a straight life. The stories are all different. Numerous guys that I have known, are sexually attracted to women, but find emotional intimacy with a woman highly intimidating. They have typically chosen

---

[65] Jones, op. cit., p. 84. Jones is quoting Byrne and Parsons "Human Sexual Orientation: The Biologic Theories Reappraised," <u>Archives of General Psychiatry</u> 50, No.3, pgs. 228-239.

[66] Satinover, <u>op.cit.</u>, p. 245.

casual sexual experiences with male strangers as a mean of escape/ release. Dangerous promiscuity has typified the majority of these dear souls. Our society's willingness to make casual sex available to "straights" or "gays" has also impacted on all of these people.

PSYCHOLOGY

Since 1973, homosexuality has not been formally recognized as a mental disorder in the Diagnostic and Statistical Manual of the American Psychological Association. However, some mental health professionals disagree; even today the majority of psychiatrists around the world continue to see same-sex attraction as signaling a mental illness.[67]

Research supports a relationship between homosexuality and personal distress. For example, the rates of depression, substance abuse and suicide are unusually high among those with a homosexual lifestyle, though clearly not all homosexuals are distressed. Some view the distress as indicative of something inherently wrong with homosexuality; others view homosexuals who are personally distressed as a reflection of societies disfavor.

Clearly those acting out a homosexual lifestyle live in very unstable relationships and engage in unusually promiscuous behavior. One study reported 28% of white homosexual males as having had 1000 or more lifetime partners by the time they were interviewed. While 79% of homosexual males reported that more than half of their sexual partners were strangers.[68] Other studies confirm similar behaviors. Lesbian behavior has been sexually promiscuous as well, but not anything like the incidents of male homosexuality.

There is a move in some gay circles toward acceptance of sexual relations with children before the legal age of consent. They argue for the replacement of words such as "pedophilia" and "child sexual

---

[67]-Ibid., p. 114-115.

[68]-Ibid., p. 109. The statistics from this study are very high, but all of the studies done report a very high incidence of casual sexual contact. Only 10% of the respondents could be classified as existing in "close coupled" relationships, which were only relatively less promiscuous.

assault" with the more neutral term "intergenerational intimacy."[69] The issue of whether these behaviors are maladaptive or adaptive revolves around whether they contribute to the person moving in a <u>valued</u> direction. What any of us consider a valued direction depends on the values and beliefs we bring to these issues. Even a discussion of "intergenerational intimacy" suggests a vastly different world-view from that of Christian ethical monotheism.

Likewise, research on whether homosexuality is pathological or a condition of moral or emotional sickness depends on the person's prior understandings of human health and morality. Research on whether homosexuality is a pathological condition, however, is not formally relevant to the moral or spiritual debate within the Church.

Ethical immorality and psychological abnormality are not the same thing, nor are they related by necessity. There is no necessary overlap between sinfulness and status as a psychopathology. Many conditions that are sins are not considered pathologies, including idolatry, pride, sorcery, lust or fornication. Many conditions that are considered pathological in our culture are not sins, including depression, bi-polar disorder or schizophrenia. The removal of homosexuality from the Diagnostic Statistical Manual list of pathologies should not intimidate the Church. The liberation of the lives of these, once embedded in the gay community, by the Lord Jesus through the instrumentality of His Church, His counselors and others outside the Church, will continue without the blessing of the American Psychological Association.

The crucial issue in determining whether or not homosexuality is to be regarded as a mental disorder is not the <u>cause</u> of the condition, but its consequences and the definition of mental disorder. Some proportion of homosexuals at any given time are satisfied with their sexual orientation, show no significant signs of psychopathology such as depression or acute anxiety and are able to function socially and occupationally with no impairment. For these people, using the criteria of psychological distress or disability homosexuality per se is not a mental disorder. Those whose only criteria are

---

[69]<u>Ibid.</u>, p. 111.

psychological reach this conclusion. If one uses a Biblical criterion it can be concluded that homosexuality is a violation of God's order of creation and is therefore a mental, moral and spiritual disorder! Some secularists, such as Dr. Charles Socarides, a psychiatrist in New York, sees homosexuality as a significant psychological disorder, violative of the psyche-sexual order inherent within our humanity and therefore treatable.[70]

The Old Testament Israelites were often in the substantial minority among their Near Eastern neighbors in asserting and living by their moral, civil and ceremonial codes. New Testament Christians were out of step with the Roman understanding of what constitutes good character. And so are contemporary followers of Jesus going to be out of step with the new paganism's concern for psychological fulfillment as the sole measure of a man or a woman in a culture of moral and spiritual relativism.

PUBLIC SENTIMENT

Abraham Lincoln once said, "In this age, in this country, public sentiment is everything. With it, nothing can fail; against it, nothing can succeed. Whoever molds public sentiment goes deeper than he who enacts statutes, or pronounces judicial decisions." Lincoln was right and wrong. Public sentiment, especially in an age of communications technology is everything. But it is not true that "with it, nothing can fail." Ultimately, the future belongs to God. The Christians of the 1st, 2nd and 3rd centuries did not mold the public sentiment. God molded character in them that withstood and overcame a pagan empire. And so the Lord God will mold us!

Some attempt to play the public sentiment card by arguing that at least 10% of the population is gay, thus homosexuality should be legalized. This statistic has consistently been shown to be based on a misinterpretation of deeply flawed research, published by Kinsey a generation ago. The recent and more credible statistics suggest that less than 3% of the male population and 2% or less of the female

---

[70] C. Socarides Homosexuality. New York: Jason Aranson, 1978.

population are homosexually active in a given year.[71] These people are often not exclusively homosexual. For many of those who would be homosexually active in one year are also heterosexually active in that same year. When combined together, men and women who manifest a <u>sustained</u> and <u>exclusive</u> commitment to homosexual practice in a lifetime might be lower than even 2%.

Probably fewer than 4% of the adult males and 2.5% of the adult females are engaged in sustained homosexual practice over a <u>significant</u> period of their adult life.[72] These people might be heterosexually active most of their lives with an interlude into homosexual relationships for a season. Then there may be a return to heterosexual relationships or to celibacy. In one study 42% of those who identified themselves as gay or bisexual men were married to women at the time they were interviewed.[73]

Clearly in the U.S. we worship at the altar of sex. Sex sells everything and sex is being sold to hundreds of millions of us! We are pre-occupied with sex, not like an adolescent dreaming but like a dieing glutton who eats and eats until his body is utterly disfigured. Pornography pumps billions of explicitly sexual images into millions of homes <u>every</u> night. It is not surprising that we would be having sex with our wife, our neighbors wife and/or husband, children, images on a screen, and finally with the beasts of our yards and pastures, all in the same month!

Whatever the statistics are as to the prevalence of homosexual activity it has <u>no</u> bearing on the morality or immorality of homosexual acts. The prevalence of adultery, divorce or child pornography has no impact on the issue of morality. This is true for Christians because we are defined not by our desires but by (1) <u>Spiritual reality</u> outside ourselves and (2) by visions of virtue and maturity from outside ourselves!

It is also <u>not</u> true that homosexuality is immoral because it is rare. If 30% of the population were homosexually active, homosexuality would not then become moral. Has divorce become more

---

[71]-<u>Ibid</u>., p. 46

[72]-<u>Ibid</u>., p. 45-46

[73]-<u>Ibid</u>., p. 41

"right" in 2006 than it was in 1953 because 10 times the number of people now divorce when compared with fifty years ago? The Judeo-Christian ethic, as set out in scripture, has <u>never</u> depended on the reported human experience to inform it of right and wrong. It has depended solely on the revealed <u>will</u> of God as understood by the believing Community! At times this ethic was socially the majority view and at other times the minority view. But faithful believers of all ages have at times stood <u>alone</u>! "For he who is in us is GREATER than he who is in the world."

DISCUSSION QUESTIONS

1. Discuss the "causes" of homosexual acts (including choice).
2. What have the sound bites regarding the "Gay Gene" done to your thinking?
3. Discuss the three disputed propositions between the gay rights lobby and the traditionalist.
4. Discuss the power of the emotional mismatch between the child and the same-sex parent to influence sexual identity.
5. Discuss the place of choice in decision-making and sexual identity formation.
6. Do you consider homosexuality normal, a mental disorder, a moral choice, a predetermined biological identity, etc.? Discuss.
7. Describe the relationship between ethical immorality and psychological abnormality, if any.
8. Does society's moral consensus determine the Christian ethic?

Addiction, Sin and Choice

J ason says to me, "I have been having sex with men for 10 years. Don't tell me it's wrong. It's who I am." But Jason's story was not one of 10 years of monogamy with one man. It was a story of sex with 65 men. The story didn't sound like freedom. It sounded like bondage. What if our addictions become so powerful that we not only can't change, we can't <u>see</u> ourselves doing anything else? What if the addiction has robbed us of <u>choice</u>, friendships and a vision of love?

ADDICTION, CHOICES AND ACCOUNTABILITY

A beautiful skylark, with an abundance of available worms in good soil and an open sky in which to fly is flying overhead one day when he looks down to see the Devil advertising "Large, juicy worms for sale!" The Devil beckons the skylark to fly down to his market. The skylark resists initially. He could easily get his own worms by simply digging, as he has done many times before. But curiosity and not a little bit of laziness finally prompts the skylark to give in to the Devil's entreaty and he lands at the Devil's market. The Devil promises a great bargain: one juicy worm – in an assortment of brilliant colors - for just one of the skylark's feathers. The worms are so attractive and so readily available that the skylark succumbs to the temptation, trading a single feather for one of the juiciest worms in the lot. The cost seemed relatively insignificant, the worm was extremely satisfying and no digging was required!

Day after day the skylark flew overhead, spotting the Devil's market and dropping down to trade feathers for a bright juicy worm. However, the skylark began to notice that the worms were no longer as satisfying as he had remembered and he began frequenting the Devil's market more often. Not only that, but the quality of the worms seemed to have diminished below even what the skylark could have gotten on his own with a little digging. Still he made the trade, until one day after trading a feather for a worm, he started to fly away only to tumble head long into the dirt, unable to fly. The skylark came to the surprising realization that in his haste he had traded away every one of his primary feathers, the very feathers needed for flight!

The skylark, created for the heavens yet now unable to fly, went back to his garden and began digging up as many worms as he could carry to bring to the Devil in order to bargain for the return of his feathers. Upon seeing the weary skylark and hearing his plea the Devil replied, "I don't do feathers for worms; I only do worms for feathers." And with an easy swoop of his hand he caught the helpless bird and tossed him into a small, rusted cage, never to be set free again. [74]

Clearly the story of the skylark is about addiction. At the beginning the skylark was free to act and each time he acted to give away his feathers he told himself he was free to act. With each successive bargain he was oblivious to the fact the he was not only losing the ability to say no but he was losing all of his feathers; He was losing the ability to fly. This is the <u>Devil's bargain</u> - always the incapacitating worms for feathers, never the redeeming of feathers for worms!

The skylark story reminds us that we already have good healthy "worms!" We just have to dig for them. God has provided all that we need! None of the addictive bright juicy worms (i.e. pornography, gluttony, drunkenness, casual sex, etc.) meet <u>any</u> of our real needs! We must "dig" for the <u>real</u> worms by trusting and obeying God. This same God designed us to <u>fly in faith, praise, prayer and play</u> and the continual glorification of God through the offering of

---

[74] I am indebted to Jeffrey Satinover op.cit. for his use of the skylark in his wonderful book, <u>Homosexuality and the Politics of Truth</u>, pages 130-133.

our bodies in daily <u>obedience</u>! "Shiny addictive worms" swallow our every thought, robbing us of flight and feathers!

The skylark lost his ability to choose. He habitually and compulsively chose the <u>Devil's bargain</u> until, when he looked in the mirror, he neither noticed nor cared that he had no feathers! For those in a promiscuous gay life style leaving the gay life style has typically been done with great difficulty, not because homosexuality is <u>inborn</u>, but because typical gay behavior is very <u>compelling</u> and more precisely <u>compulsive</u>! Let me be clear here: addiction is any <u>compulsive</u>, habitual behavior that limits the freedom of human desire. The attachment or nailing of desire to specific objects like homosexual orgasm, is at the center of this addiction.

Choice when applied to habitual thinking and behaviors is imprecise. The biology of a <u>habit</u> has to do with the <u>plasticity</u> of the brain. The brain is literally rutted out by habitual behavior. Biologically patterns of choices tend to be self-reinforcing. What begins relatively freely becomes less so as time goes on. We become <u>addicted</u> to the chemical high, the orgasm or the food. Gerald May says that the word "behavior" is especially important in this definition, for it indicates that <u>action</u> is essential to addiction. The *attachment of desire* is the underlying process that results in addictive behavior. Desire attaches to a homosexual <u>act</u> that repeated again and again becomes very addictive.[75]

Disciples of Jesus understand that within addiction is also <u>idolatry</u>! We begin worshipping the <u>feelings, highs, and orgasms</u>, i.e. the shiny worms. Those who worship Yahweh, the Holy God, can discern the element of idolatry within the compulsive, driven, addictive behavior. The believer discerns the manner in which the idolatry of addiction removes us from a real relationship with God and other people! The word "sin" brings the addiction into relationship with God. The word "addiction" only describes our relationship to the object of our addiction or to our own body chemicals.

Though sexual addiction "takes us over" we remain accountable for our actions. We made choices or at least at one time we did. We may now feel as if we have no choice. But we do. Otherwise

---

[75] Gerald May, <u>Grace and Addiction</u> (San Francisco: Harper Collins, 1988) pgs 24-25.

we lose accountability for ourselves and we become little pathetic caricatures of ourselves. In spite of habit, compulsive behavior and addiction we are still free to choose to act in opposition to our sexual bondage. A good place to begin may be a modified first three steps of the AA program:

1. We admit that we are powerless over homosexual addiction, that our lives have become unmanageable.
2. We have come to believe that the Lord God can restore us to sanity.
3. We have made a decision to turn our will and our lives over to the care of the Lord God.

The humble confessions made among other confessing sinners, including an urgent request that the Spirit of God live in our bodies, gives us the space and the power to begin to choose obedience. It is a long obedience in one direction. It is a humble beginning, but it is much better than the pitiful humiliation of the addiction. The power to choose life can return to our bodies as we submit ourselves to the truth about ourselves, to a community of fellow strugglers and to the Lord God. Liberation from bondage is what Jesus the Christ our Lord came to do among us! (Mark 10:45)

Abstinence from homosexual acts is not the cure, but the precondition of the cure. The distress of abstinence is even greater because the usual routes of escape from our personal distress have been sealed off. To be healed our pain <u>must</u> get worse. The underlying distress that fueled the addiction gets worse as we practice abstinence from the addiction. Slowly we begin to "plant flowers" in our lives -- new habits, new relationships, new beliefs that become alternative means of dealing with distress.

Before going on, I must say that this agonizing valley of painful abstinence must be brought to the Body of Christ. We must be in a "New Family" of intimate relationships with those who will weep with us, pray for us and talk to us about real life. (1 Corinthians 12) This is not just a work for professionals but for the entire beautiful Body of Christ. Loneliness and depression are lifted by real, present relationships where strugglers sit and share their lives – pain and joy. It is crucial that we say out loud, "I am depressed. I am in pain." We must come around those who are battling homosexual addictions, providing a powerful place and a safe place!

Addictions usually come from individually heightened temptation and a willingness to use alcohol, sexual orgasm, food, etc. as a solution to being human. In Samuel Johnson's words, "He who makes a beast of himself gets rid of the pain of being a man." No one is exempt from this broken means of being human – no one is altogether whole in his capacity to love and be loved. All of us are in need of the deep work of healing, forgiving and restoring that our Lord seeks to establish in the sexuality of His people. This healing begins with turning to the Lord God, away from the idols, taking responsibility for all of our actions, walking in authentic holiness, confessing when we fail, living ALWAYS in HOPE, and doing it all within the knit together community of Jesus the Lord!

A CHRISTIAN VIEW OF ADDICTION AND NORMALCY

The Christian notion of sin, simply put, means the entire world is not as it should be. Rebellion, loneliness, one-night stands, bondages, diseases and death – in a very real sense what we call human has become inhuman. What we now call normal is in fact abnormal. What we now call natural is in fact unnatural. Sin has become pleasurable and self-reinforcing to the point of compulsions and addictions so that sin now seems human, normal and natural to us![76]

When a married man says, "Sex with my girlfriend feels right," what he means is that it feels human, normal and natural, as though that give him license for his actions. The implication, of course, is that his "inner feelings", bound within his own addictive world, take preeminence over all external logic, reason, spirituality or holiness. It is not just the gay community who makes arguments for the spiritually inhuman, abnormal and unnatural acts as though they have now become human, normal and natural. Divorce and remarriage, greed and gluttony, for example, are excused every day in the Church because they feel normal, human, and natural. In all of these

---

[76] Satinover, op.cit., pages 146-168.

instances sin has become <u>self-reinforcing</u>, leading to what the Bible calls a <u>snare</u>.

"The evil deeds of a wicked man <u>ensnare</u> him. The cords of his sin hold him fast. He will die for a lack of discipline led astray by his own folly." (Proverbs 5:22)

2 Peter 2:19 says, "A man is a slave to whatever has mastered him." When mastered by desires and no longer able to desire something else, <u>denial</u> tends to take over as a mechanism subverting any residual suspicion that escape is even desirable. "I am not an alcoholic! Though I drink 70 beers a week, manifest severe mood swings and live my life thinking about purchasing, gulping down and recovering from beer, I am not an alcoholic." That is denial on the way to delusion.

A frightening vice can become a virtue. "Just a way to have a little fun." Getting what we want <u>all</u> the time has become a virtue. "The heart is deceitful above all things and beyond cure. Who can understand it?" (Jeremiah 17:9) When we wake up in the middle of addiction our psyches have already been shaped by our behavior. It has been burned into the synaptic connections of the brain. "Judah's sin is engraved with an iron tool, inscribed with a flint point, on the tablets of their hearts and on the horns of their altars." (Jeremiah 17:11)

The Apostle Paul refers to the body of death in Romans 7:24. "What a wretched man I am! Who will rescue me from this *body of death?*" This passage refers to the death sentence that was carried out under Imperial Rome. A dead body was strapped to the back of a condemned man from which he could not free himself, however he might struggle. In time the putrefaction of the corpse spread and ate away his tissues as well, slowly killing him. So it is that sin eats away at the <u>purposes</u> of God for our physical bodies. In a fallen world a sinful body of addicted death appears natural. But when the Spirit lives in us, we envision our bodies as temples of God and we see sin for what it is!

The sinful body of addicted death may include some genetic and environmental components and it almost certainly includes choice and addiction components, but the exact components of homosexuality in our bodies does not remove it <u>one bit</u> from the domain of mental choice. In it's genetic, familial, psychological and choice components homosexual impulses and behaviors are no different than many other "natural" behaviors the Lord calls sin. It is important here to note that Jesus was once asked to speculate as to the past: "Who sinned, this man or another?" (John 9:2,3) Jesus refused to dwell on the past but instead spoke of the man's condition as an occasion for the purposes of God to be <u>realized</u>! The real issue for all of us addicted sinners goes not to the past but to God's purposes for our futures! Whatever the reason for our failings, are we living out God's purposes for our lives?

The modern mind opposes the Christian view of fallenness, arguing, "Whatever IS is right." The Christian view of sin was stated simply in the movie "Grand Canyon" when one character exclaimed "This ain't the way it's supposed to be." The "new pagan" considers the demand that we live against our "natures" as merely foolish. They misinterpret the Christian view of sin as an anti-body religion that rejects all pleasure. They see as totally cruel the judgment that supposedly falls on us for not being willing to resist our genetic and/ or psychological influences. For the new pagan our bodies are ours to do with as we please so long as we do not harm anyone.

I have preached the funerals of men who contracted AIDS through anal sex. Although current scientific research has documented that the physiology of anal intercourse is inherently dangerous, I have yet to have anyone step up to me and claim responsibility for contributing to the death of these men who have died. We continue to redefine our humanity until there is no accountability for any sex act no matter how dangerous. We are coming to believe that the culprit is our own body fluids!

The homosexual lobby turns any repression of sexual impulses into the victimization of a helpless repressor. The fact is that as long as I celebrate sexuality as God intended it and do not become a body hater or shamer, repression of at least some of my sexual impulses is a very healthy thing to do. Without some repression there is no community; there are no Fathers - only one-night stand semen donors; there is no family; there is no civilization!

In comparison, consider the heterosexual NFL professional athlete who fathers countless children out of wedlock. Why is it that we don't consider a sexually addicted professional athlete an unaccountable victim when we demand that he stop his promiscuity and pay his child support? His heterosexual genetics, family experiences, psychological conditioning and choices have taught him that such addictive irresponsible behavior is normal, healthy and natural. Yet we expect him as a moral agent to cease and desist from such irresponsible behavior.

He is not a victim, but a magnificent child of God addicted to sins and in desperate need of the forgiveness at Christ's cross and the power of the Spirit to break sin's authority over his life and deliver him from his bondage! The fact that he has the option to marry a woman may make his recovery easier, but it doesn't guarantee that he'll be capable of holding marriage together. Furthermore, since he has <u>learned</u> that one woman can never satisfy his fantasy and/or ego world, the fact that he is married typically does not make the breaking of the bondage any <u>easier</u>! Yet he, like his brother or sister who struggles with homosexuality, is accountable for his actions.

Two weeks before Gerald died of AIDS he had contracted from anal intercourse during a one night stand, I came to see him. He had asked me to preach his funeral. As we were discussing what had transpired the night he contracted AIDS, his Dad overheard us and said, "I blame it on him," referring to his son's "lover". Gerald quickly shot back, "I did it, Dad. I got myself plastered drunk and then had sex with this guy. It was my fault."

Gerald's refusal to blame coupled with his willingness to say "I did it" made a lasting impression on me. His Daddy was in such pain as he watched his son die in that house that he became temporarily unable to acknowledge his son's culpability. Yet his son Gerald said, "I did it" before the throne of God, pled the blood of Jesus and was empowered by the Holy Spirit to confess Jesus as Savior and Lord until his last breath. The Lord comes to those who say "Son of David have mercy on me. I did it!"

Many unchurched people came to Gerald's funeral. His witness to the Lamb of God permeated the room. The victory of the kingdom reverberated across a room full of those who came in not knowing their spiritual addresses.

All of us can still cry out to God and to the community of Jesus' friends, asking for help to overcome. Too often we have stupidly flown with the Skylark! Now it's time to get up on the eagle's wings and ride the painful ride out of addiction. It will hurt! But the pain will be full of joyful meaning. We were made to fly! We were not made to grovel like pigs in sexual addictions, food addictions or any other addiction. Jesus is a bondage-breaker! Let Him break your bondage though the instrumentality of the Holy Spirit and the Body of Christ.

DISCUSSION QUESTIONS

1. Explore and discuss ways in which you've "traded feathers for worms."
2. In a very practical sense, what have you lost from "the devil's trade?" Where should you be flying?
3. Why do we want "juicy worms" when we already have all the worms we need?
4. Define addiction.
5. Discuss the differences and similarities between sin and addiction.
6. Has sin ever felt normal, natural and human to you? Explain.
7. Discuss the AA steps out of addiction.

Normal, Sinful or a Sickness?

⟨℥⟩

If Andrew Sullivan, the most articulate advocate of homosexual marriage in America today, cannot describe homosexual behavior as normal in his book <u>Virtually Normal</u>, then what is it? Sin? Sickness? None of the above? Does it really matter what words we use to describe homosexual behavior? Absolutely. Words not only pack tremendous power in and of themselves but they also connote the feelings, beliefs and agendas of the speaker, whether intentional or not. They often give definition and clarity to what is sometime hidden behind sentence structure and composition. For example, both homophobic bigots and gay liberationists throw the word "queer" around and may even elicit equal amounts of passion from it's use, but each has chosen the word for completely different reasons and with completely different connotations.

Normal, sin or a sickness? These words used to describe homosexuality point to dramatically different worldviews! In no instance should the Church be interested in name-calling or stereotyping. But we should be interested in putting homosexuality within the context of our worldview, our view of what is real – both the glory and the tragedy of it!

VIRTUALLY NORMAL

Andrew Sullivan, the Roman Catholic editor of the journal, the New Republic from 1991 through 1996, in his 1995 book <u>Virtually Normal</u>, makes arguably the strongest case in print for the legalization of homosexual marriage. Sullivan distinguishes his position from among those of both the Christian prohibitionist and the gay-rights liberationist, as well as from among the socially conservative and the socially liberal. Only the liberal, however, would agree, even in principle, with Sullivan's advocacy of homosexual marriage.

The quality of Sullivan's arguments and the passion with which he advocates homosexual marriage reminds us that we must deal with all men and women as unique individuals. For example, many gay liberationists led by Michael Foucalt have no use for marriage, much less homosexual marriage. The stereotyping of all homosexuals under one designation is clearly a <u>dishonest</u> and <u>unloving</u> act against people such as Foucalt and Sullivan.

Sullivan acknowledges that he had a very close relationship with his Mother and a distant somewhat warring relationship with his Father. "And in all this, I suppose, I follow a typical pattern of homosexual development."[77] Clearly, he is implicitly acknowledging a brokenness inherent within his relationships to his parents. Sullivan never argues that homosexuality is normal. He simply says, "The homosexual experience may be deemed an illness, a disorder, a privilege or a curse; it may be deemed worthy of a 'cure,' rectified, embrace or endured. <u>But it exists</u>."[78] This is Sullivan's argument. He makes it in the prologue to the book and everything he says subsequently is based on it. Even in his telling of his own story of what he calls his orientation as a homosexual at age ten, he is not arguing that he is <u>normal</u>, but that he is what he is, a man with a homosexual identity.

The homosexual experience, for Sullivan, "occurs independently of the form of its expression; it is based upon the mysterious and unstable area where sexual desire and emotional longing meet; it reaches into the core of what makes a human being who he or she is. The origins of homosexuality are remarkably mysterious and probably due to a mixture of some genetic factors and very early childhood development (before the age of 5 or 6). But those arguments are largely irrelevant for the discussion that follows. The truth is that,

---

[77] Andrew Sullivan, <u>Virtually Normal</u>. (New York, Random House, 1995), p. 93.

[78]-<u>Ibid.</u>, p.7

for the overwhelming majority of adults, the condition of homo-sexuality is as <u>involuntary</u> as heterosexuality is for heterosexuals. Such an orientation is evident from the very beginning of a person's emotional identity. These are the only <u>unavoidable premises</u> of the argument that follows."[79] Everything flows from this human, almost normal, orientation!

Sullivan attaches singular significance to Ludwig Wittgenstein's words, "One can only describe here and say: this is what human life is like." In other words, Sullivan's description of his human broken life supersedes in importance the words of scripture, the Church and any other spiritual authority. Furthermore, Sullivan argues, given the unalterable nature of our sexual identities and the centrality of our sexual identities to our humanity, the Church <u>must</u> expand her view of marriage to include homosexual marriage and thus pastor her homosexual children into Holy matrimony. Sullivan passion-ately argues that our longing to express our love for our lovers, same sex or opposite sex, <u>must</u> be expressed and <u>should</u> be expressed in marriage.

Sullivan redefines marriage to include homosexual marriage arguing that the traditional biblical-ecclesiastical notions of marriage do not preclude a lesbian or homosexual marital commitment. He says, "It is my view that in same-sex marriage, adultery should be as anathema as it is in heterosexual marriage."[80]

Sullivan is correct when he says that an attraction towards homosexual relationships from childhood has been the experience of some. Yet he ignores the ambivalence, the yes and no, reported by millions of homosexual strugglers. In other words, the "orienta-tion" is <u>not nearly</u> as fixed and powerful in most same-sex strugglers as Sullivan claims. Our sexual identities are not entirely involun-tary, but are heavily influenced, even in adulthood, by environment and behavior choices. Sullivan ignores the dynamic, fragile nature of most developing sexual identities.[81]

---

[79]-<u>Ibid.</u>, p. 7

[80]-<u>Ibid.</u>, p.221

[81] Satinover, op.cit., p. 168-220. Satinover, a Christian psychiatrist, discusses secular and Christian treatment modalities in this section.

Sullivan's declaration that attempts at change of the "homosexual identity" have ended in defeat ignores the multiplied thousands of documented changes occurring within the last twenty years.[82] I have personally witnessed these changes in the lives of five young men in the church where I pastor. It happens! Sullivan never references the liberating power of the Lord within His Church in which the Spirit of God works through the open confessions of believers who become family to one-another, providing the Fathers, Mothers, sisters and brothers we didn't get the first time. It is here that <u>change</u> is occurring for <u>all</u> those who follow Jesus, not just homosexuals! Sullivan only knows "what is!" He does not speak of what <u>has happened</u> in Christ, what God has for those who love him <u>now</u> and what fulfillment all of us will know when all things are brought to fulfillment in Christ! Can anybody speak authoritatively regarding normal human behavior without first speaking of the Creator and His purposes?

Sullivan argues that if homosexuality is involuntary and unchangeable (which I dispute), it is at worst "morally neutral." It is on this foundation that all of his arguments rest. Yet, if we are born into a Fallen World – biologically, psychologically and socially, and we are, then the product of that fallenness is not morally neutral. The fact that we have been sinned against by abusive, controlling Mothers, and negligent, distant Fathers, does not produce "neutral" fruit. As a result of this Fallen World, we also make sinful behavior decisions. These are not morally neutral. This understanding that "whatever is" is not necessarily right, should lead us to cry out for liberation! We are not free to just go with whatever "identity" our physical parents perpetrated on us. We will then almost inevitably solidify our fallen mindset by "acting it out" – thus indelibly burning into our psyches the ravages of sin. What kind of legacy do we then leave?

Sullivan's arguments for marriage include his advocacy of sex acts within homosexual marriage, prohibited by scripture, that creates enormous health risks for the participants. He redefines marriage as the commitment of two loved ones, discarding the Christian notion of a sexually complementing (man-wife) lifetime covenant. Christian

---

[82] Ibid.

marriage is <u>reinvented</u> so as to allow him and others with the same story to live out their humanity with the Sacramental Blessing of the Lord and His Church for their marriages. Whenever we reinvent the teachings of Christ we are behaving in bold and risky ways that invite ultimate disaster into our lives. Not only that, by what authority do any of us ignore the clear teachings of Scripture, placing our "longings, our wild humanity" above the Lord and His clear will?

Andrew Sullivan, though mistaken on significant issues, appears to be a man of some honor, integrity and restraint. His life, like many who agree with him, manifests a measure of integrity and courage. The criticisms I make of his positions as referenced above are not the same criticism that can be leveled against the sexual promiscuity of gay liberationists. Sullivan is neither an advocate for nor excusing of a promiscuous gay lifestyle. He is a serious advocate for homosexual marriage and for the right to live a sexual life inside a marital commitment.

Jonathan Rauch, in his book <u>Gay marriage</u> (2004) argues that gay marriage is the best public policy for gays, straights and for marriage. Rauch contends that since sexual orientation is fixed at birth gays constitute a class of people that are being discriminated against. According to Rauch, failure to legalize homosexual marriage constitutes a violation of the social contract afforded to all Americans by their citizenship in a liberal democracy.

Yet Rauch fails to acknowledge the homosexual community's division over the concept of sexual orientation. Whereas Rauch considers sexual orientation a biologically determined essence that cannot be changed short of grave danger to the psyche and personhood, others within the gay community hold to the social construct view that human sexuality is plastic and flexible. According to his view one learns to think of oneself as gay or lesbian depending on the social context. Many of those holding this view advocate getting beyond the distinction between gay and straight, forming a new, liberated, sexually fluid bisexuality. These people within the gay community reject the idea of same-sex marriage, finding it oppressive and tolerating it only as a transitional moment toward the eventual abolition of marriage.

Given this ongoing debate, is society being asked to redefine marriage for an "oppressed minority" whose sexual orientation is allegedly an unchanging essence, or is it being asked to not only redefine marriage but its entire understanding of sexuality – a change that could usher in a new flexible bisexuality, etc. that would transcend the poles of homosexual and heterosexual? [83] The latter alternative would seek to abolish marriage as a legal institution.

I take Andrew Sullivan and Jonathan Rauch at their word when they insist that they are simply seeking to extend the good of marriage, that they bear no interest in injuring the traditional family. Yet in addition to the objections stated above, their argument does in fact erode the very meaning of marriage so as to make untenable any resistance in principle to polygamy, alliances of widows or brothers and sisters, claiming no erotic or sexual relation, but seeking the financial advantage of marriage.[84]

Mel White, a former speechwriter and ghostwriter for several noteworthy public Christian personalities, including Pat Robertson and Jerry Falwell, after twenty-five years of marriage, recently announced his homosexual orientation and his same-sex lover. White claims to remain an evangelical Christian. He contends that Scripture does not anticipate the plight of those who from day one are sexually oriented toward homosexuality. He also contends that the documented changes of sexual orientation from a homosexual orientation to a heterosexual orientation are all a hoax. The arguments in his book are very similar to those Sullivan, a Roman Catholic, makes in Virtually Normal. White, for forty years, hid his struggle from the Church, before finally publicly declaring himself gay.[85]

---

[83] Browning and Marguardt, op.cit., p.50

[84] Hadley Arkes, "The Family and the Laws", The Meaning of Marriage, Robert P. George and Jean Bethke Elshtain, eds. (Dallas, Texas. Spence Publishing Company 2006), p. 127

[85] Mel White, Stranger at the Gate, (Penguin Books, New York, 1995).

SIN VERSES SICKNESS

I argue for the Biblical diagnosis of sin, which preserves our awareness of the God dynamics within our broken behavior. I understand my story as well as Sullivan, Rauch and White to be laced with the dynamics of sin. The notion of sin or fallenness, in all of its dimensions, points to God as Creator of our humanity. It is against the background of man's dignity and glory as God's creation that the notion of sin appears as a tragic rebellion, a state of separation, a brokenness received in our biologies, psychologies and families, a behavioral choice as well as an oppressive addiction. Reference to sin does not rule out describing a behavior as a sickness or an addiction.

SIN IN THE WIDER CULTURE

One of the most obvious fruit of our present rebellion is that we now determine what is right and what is wrong. At any given time we may be breaking 8 or 10 of the Ten Commandments, but we don't go to therapy to stop; we got to therapy to feel good about breaking the commandments. For example, we often seek therapy to "get over" a divorce, not to repent of what led to the divorce!

There's only two commandments now: "Thou shalt feel good about thy self all the time, " and "Thou shalt tolerate your brothers behavior, without judging him, as long as his behavior does not harm you." As slaves of sin (addicts), apart from Christ, we become comfortable in denial. We consider ourselves free from the consequences of choice. Since Freud we have increasingly considered conscience and guilt as culturally relative and derived from nothing more absolute than learned restrictions that lead to internal conflicts passed on from one generation to the next.

In other words, guilt is a useless emotion! We typically deal with guilt by loosening restrictions as archaic and arbitrary. We typically only accommodate guilt or restriction when it maintains the social order. For example, murder or political treason or fraud (if it divests thousands of people of billions of dollars as in the Enron case) cannot be tolerated because of their impact on the stability of the <u>social order</u>. Yet at the same time the Fox network produces a television show called Temptation Island, which tempts the already immoral who live with their girl friends to commit adultery and/or fall in love with another hand picked seducer. This sort of sin is not considered sinful because, according to today's standards, it does not disrupt the social order. Clearly it not only harms many of the participants, it also reveals the depravity – the hollowness – the self-worship within us!

The casting off of restraint has not always led to easy consciences. Our consciences still condemn us, even though we say we do not believe in an eternally binding moral law, we <u>are</u> hurt when relationships die and a commitment is broken. We desperately work at <u>suppressing the truth</u>, at not knowing what we know! Yet apart from a Holy God who graciously cares for us we become even more rebellious and bitter. We act out in justified self-centeredness, contending that the betrayals we suffer justify the betrayal we will perpetrate! There is no end to such behavior. Guilt – real guilt – exists. It is there because we violated not only the heart and law of God but we violate one another.

A judge friend of mine in Tarrant County, Texas who has been on the bench for about a year was recently asked how he liked his job. He gave a "thumbs up" with one significant complaint. He said, "Thousands of people came through this courtroom this past year, and almost all of them <u>blamed</u> the opposing party for their troubles! Nobody took personal responsibility for what they had done. Blame, blame, blame! No <u>personal conviction</u>. All of this shatters our families." He found this pervading unaccountability very discouraging. Conviction of sin and acknowledgment of personal accountability stops the blaming and starts the rebuilding!

HOMOSEXUAL SIN

Homosexual sin partakes of this <u>wider culture of sin</u>. Homosexual sin is <u>not</u> a special depraved form of sin. It is a socially contemporary manifestation of our separation from a Holy God, and our resultant confusion within our impulse-driven lives. Homosexual sins partake of the wider sexual idolatry that worships at the altar of orgiastic pleasure. The narcissism (self-centeredness) of homosexuality is no more deadly than the radical self-centeredness of the heterosexual libertine who physically produces babies he never intends to nurture as a Father. The very idea that he should weigh the possibility of pregnancy before he has sexual intercourse is not taken seriously. The idols whisper in our ears, "You <u>must</u> satisfy your instincts." The best this man can do is buy a good prophylactic in the bathroom at the convenience store before going to have sex with a woman he may never see again.

Promiscuous homosexual activity occurs in the same irresponsible culture. We are having anal intercourse or oral sex with another man, not because we may, but because we <u>must</u>. At least this is in our minds. The orgiastic release is god, however dangerous it may be. Most of these people have had sexual relations with opposite sex lovers.[86] But they still call themselves homosexual because they never found the highest high with a <u>woman</u>.[87] The validation for casual sex acts is in the orgiastic pinnacle, not in the unitive binding of two committed soul mates.

Those who contend for a same-sex marriage redefine marriage much like the millions of Christian heterosexuals who have redefined marriage as they divorced their wives and ran to their new soul mates! In both instances Biblical man-woman covenant marriage is being reinvented and ultimately discarded. Now, given the divorce rate, serial monogamous commitments have replaced man-woman life-long covenants as the cultural norm.

Given the sin culture we inhabit, sickness is not the fundamental diagnosis of homosexual acts. Rather, we get sick because of the dimensions of sin among us – rebellion, a God void, being sinned against, a fallen biology and psychology, bad choices. Homosexuality is an illness only in the sense that it reflects a disease of men and women who rebel and do as they please. Homosexuality does not rank anywhere near the center of what the Bible calls sin.

---

[86] Stanton op. cit., pgs. 141-146.

[87] Again and again homosexual behavior has been justified to me by the reasoning that heterosexual sex is simply not the "highest high." This is consistent with the New Paganism spirituality of the self. The self is now God!

Sin is exchanging the worship of the Creator for images in rebellion against the Creator, and then living out the bad fruit of that rebellion (Romans 1:18-32). Homosexual sin, one bad fruit of rebellion, points to the poverty of our spiritual life in the same way that all sin unwittingly points to the Creator Lord who made us for something better.

When we refer to homosexuality or heterosexual immorality as illnesses we are not completely wrong. We do get sick physically, spiritually and emotionally. We contract diseases because we are outside the covenant protection of the Lord God. We become addicted <u>within</u> our sexual idolatries, our brains groan for the very titillation and high that will kill our brains! We lose sensitivities to real sexual love making within a long-term commitment. The word illness or disease indicates that <u>foreign</u> bodies have penetrated our immune systems and are now at war with the purposeful healthy functions of our bodies. And that is true.

LIBERATION AND HEALING

Yet disease is not the fundamental diagnosis. For we do business first not with the creation but with the Creator. We often get sick because we sin and because we've been sinned against. But we should not play the helpless victim. Such is beneath our dignity as divine image-bearers. We must breathe in God and consider our own sin now: our attitudes, habits, feelings and relationships that enslave us every day. Consider that although we have received a fallen biology, psychology and sociology and have been sinned against from childhood through adulthood, we have also received magnificent body-souls from the Creator. We are fallen, but not ruined; we are still God's image bearers. Remember also that Jesus Christ is ALIVE, ready to not only forgive us all of our sins, but to also liberate us from the compulsive grip of sin.

"Do you not know that the wicked will not inherit the kingdom of God? Do not be deceived: neither the sexually immoral nor idolaters nor adulterers nor male prostitutes nor homosexual offenders nor thieves nor the greedy nor drunkards nor slanders nor swindlers will inherit the kingdom of God. <u>And that is what some of you were</u>. But you were <u>washed, you were sanctified, you were justified in the name of the Lord Jesus Christ and by the Spirit of Our God.</u>"[88]

There is liberation in relationship under the Lord Jesus Christ through the power of the Spirit of God <u>within the Body of Christ</u>! Clearly homosexual sin is <u>not</u> unique. Jesus liberates all sinners from idolatry, from loneliness, from guilt, from shame and from all the compulsive powers of disobedience! Yet, in our time the biblical faith and it's attendant standard of morality <u>feels unnatural</u>. And so we run from the Biblical pictures of <u>morality</u>, <u>redemption</u> and <u>community</u>!

Stubbornly we return to our excuse, "I am suffering from a disease" and therefore reject any guilt rather than accept that what we're suffering from is a morally defective choice. And because I am now not guilty, I need not rebel against that guilt toward God by insisting on my right to continue as I was. Because I have redefined the problem as a disease, which is morally neutral, I can acknowledge my problem. This analysis ignores the fact that at some point, possibly at many points, we <u>willfully</u> chose the forbidden behavior. Also this analysis refuses to acknowledge the fact that we refused to bring our guilt feelings <u>before God</u> who would not only convict us of our sin, but also <u>forgive us</u> in one supernatural sweep of divine life. How could it be true that the illness diagnosis that removes the notion of sin is more on target than the sin diagnosis that <u>includes</u> an understanding of disease? Maybe we want it to be an illness for then we don't have to grapple with the fact that within our addiction there is often idolatry, rebellion and arrogant deceptions that refuse to encounter a Holy God!

To compound the issue, those who redefine their sin within the context of "sickness" have typically found it easier than the confessing sinner to find mercy – albeit, a false mercy without judgment - and compassion from the Church. Why do we have trouble extending compassion for people who make bad moral choices? Is it

---

[88] 1 Corinthians 6:9-11

because we <u>feel superior</u> to them? If so, it's only because we are not in relationship with Christ who helps us become aware of our own sinful choices and of the fact that <u>we are forgiven</u>! This forgiveness is only possible through the atoning Messiah. It is Jesus the Christ who showed compassion on those locked into compulsive sinful behaviors and who teaches us to do the same. Our own personal redemption stories have taught us that redemption involves not only a great Divine grace, spiritual empowerment, and tight-knit community, but also requires an enormous personal effort including <u>pain</u>, <u>suffering</u>, <u>humility</u> and <u>moral failures</u>!

Addictions and deeply embedded compulsive behavior patterns differ from true illness in that their <u>progressive</u> alteration of the brain is directed by <u>choices</u>, especially initial choices, reinforced by the progressive erosion of the ability to choose differently. Compulsions include elements of choice and disease. It is a way of life in which a <u>free moral life</u> is undone. For those who come to Christ out of the world, locked in compulsive behavior, they must first understand that their addiction includes idolatry. Those who have not known the transcendent Lord have no concept of the idolatrous dimension of compulsive behavior. Only as they come to know God through Christ do they begin to see their compulsive behavior as the altar at which they <u>once worshipped</u>!

PROPER JUDGMENTS

Those who are called to true compassion for those locked in compulsive homosexual behavior make judgments as to the sinfulness of the homosexual acts, but they do not judge as one who has no sin, refusing to see their own. They do not <u>condemn</u> when they make judgments. Paul's letters to Christians and Jesus' words to his disciples were full of <u>judgment</u> as to right and wrong, holiness and unholiness, freedom and bondage, the wise and unwise.[89] But unless the believer was in open rebellion, there was <u>never</u> condemnation or <u>excommunication</u>!

---

[89] 1 Corinthians 5, 6, 10 and 11 are examples of proper judgment.

In the Church we should understand that compulsive sins committed by those who are not in rebellion against God, but who seek in their weakness to live in open confession are never a justification for rejection of such a person. "If a man says he does not commit sins he is a liar. But if he confesses his sin god is faithful and just to forgive him." (1 John 1:1-81)

Therefore, for us true compassion requires acknowledgement of what sin consists in, but coupled with an unwillingness to condemn the person based on our own knowledge of our own salvation from sin. If we know we are saved though we still commit sins, we will not only speak discerning judgment on fellow same-sex strugglers in Christ, but on ourselves! We will also ask those who struggle with compulsive homosexual behavior in Christ to speak into our lives the merciful judgments of God!

It is within a community of hope, compassion and truth that self-discipline and accountability become important components in the healing of all forms of sinful, compulsive, and addictive behavior. Apart from hope and compassion, self-discipline and accountability collapse. The entire pilgrimage of repentance and behavioral change from addiction to freedom, from idolatry to God, often includes much pain and sorrow on the way to a final victory! This journey must be full of hope and compassion mediated by the Church.

The power of authentic, hopeful Christian community cannot be overestimated. More than 20 years ago an acknowledgment appeared in the American Journal of Psychology regarding the healing of eleven formerly homosexual men within a community of unconditional love without explicit treatment and/or long term psychotherapy. This type of healing may be much more common than previously thought.[90] These amazing healings are happening within authentic Spirit-empowered Christian community in which the real, healthy dynamics of the family of God shape all of our lives!

Too often homosexual strugglers are caught in the homosexuality vs. Christianity vice-grip; they hear sermons preached that either condemn homosexuality along with the homosexual or they

---

[90] Satinover, op. cit., pgs. 141-146.

hear a doctrine of unqualified acceptance portrayed as tolerance and enlightenment. Either way, they remain unaware of the possibility of sexual redemption. Sexual redemption in Christ is possible through the loving support of a community that embodies the Gospel of God's love.

For more than three thousand years the ethics of the Holy Lord of Israel and the Church have stood opposed to the beliefs and practices of the paganism surrounding her. And for more than three thousand years, the Holy God of Israel has been concerned with two things: intimacy with His people and their walk in His holy ways.

The cure of a soul that progresses over a lifetime is more than the alteration of particular symptoms. It involves going toward the divinely ordained shape that God intended for us from the beginning and that now seems largely unnatural. Long-term homosexual behavior may be difficult to modify because it involves innate impulses and <u>repeatedly reinforced sinful choices</u> by which <u>sinful activities</u> become embedded in the brain and "engraved on the heart." But these dynamics as we have seen are not unique to homosexuality.

It is crucial that we properly diagnose the problem. But then it is equally crucial that all of us compulsive sinners walk out our redemption together in the power of the Lord!

DISCUSSION QUESTIONS

1. Give an example of homosexual stereotyping and discuss how that affects your view of sexual redemption for homosexuals.
2. Discuss the strengths and weaknesses of Sullivan's argument in <u>Virtually Normal.</u>
3. Do you consider homosexuality a sin, a sickness or both? Discuss.
4. Discuss the dimensions of sin as referenced in this chapter.
5. Where does homosexuality fit within a Christian worldview and a Christian view of creation, sin and redemption?
6. Discuss the relationship of sin to sickness and vice-versa as related to homosexuality.

7. Why do we often have more compassion for "sick" people than we do for sinners? Define "sick" within this context.

Exegesis of the Biblical Passages
Genesis 19:1-29

"Isn't Sodomy the worst sin in the Bible?"

"Why do we follow the prescriptions of Leviticus against homosexuality but ignore many of its other prescriptions, including the forbidding of marital intercourse during the menstrual period?"

"Wasn't Paul addressing the 'gay' sins of his time in a manner that is not relevant for 'loving monogamous gays' today?"

I do hear a few of these types of questions about the Bible today. But on balance I don't hear many questions regarding the Bible. The traditionalists seem to already know all the answers and those who would revise our reading of the Bible put little weight on scriptural authority. I find the Bible's "position" on these matters surprisingly "out of step" with the church and the world!

Lets take a good look at the Biblical passages within the Old and New Testaments that specifically discuss homosexuality.

SODOM

In Genesis 19:1-29, the Sodom and Gomorrah passage describes the men of Sodom pounding on Lot's door. The NIV translates 19:5 as follows: "They called to Lot, 'Where are the men who came to you tonight? Bring them out to us so that we can have sex (*yada*) with them.'" Later the text says, "They kept bringing pressure on

Lot and moved forward to break down the door." (vs.9) The men of Sodom apparently intended to gang rape Lot's two angel visitors.

The notion of homosexual gang rape in Genesis 19 violated the norms of all ancient Near Eastern societies. Clearly, this instance of sin is a part of the sin of Sodom. Yet neither this text nor the several references to Sodom in the Old Testament mention homosexual sin as the sin of Sodom. (See Isa. 3:9, Jer. 23:14, Lam. 4:6, Zeph. 2:8-9). For example, Ezekiel 16:49 says, "Now this was the sin of your sister Sodom: She and her daughters were <u>arrogant</u>, <u>overfed</u>, and <u>unconcerned</u>; they did not help the poor and needy. They were <u>haughty</u> and did <u>detestable</u> things before me." Homosexual gang rape was just one sin among several.

Therefore, we cannot conclude that the Lord God's intention to destroy Sodom and Gomorrah was primarily the result of homosexual sin in Sodom. It is interesting to note, contextually speaking, that the Lord God tells Abraham of a coming judgment on Sodom (Ch. 18) *before* the story of the attempted homosexual rape of Chapter 19. Genesis never catalogues the sins of Sodom. The Genesis context, Chapters 18 and 19, is dominated by Abraham's prayers for Sodom as God's covenant partner and by the fact that the Lord God "remembered Abraham" and therefore saved Lot from the destruction of Sodom.

Certainly, as Jude 7 says, "Sodom and Gomorrah gave themselves up to sexual immorality and perversion." Yet even here the literal rendering of the Greek word translated perversion says, "*and went after other flesh.*" The phrase "went after other flesh" refers to their pursuit of nonhuman (i.e. angelic) "flesh."[91] Thus, technically speaking, it is impossible to construe Jude 7 as a condemnation of homosexual desire. Homosexual desire is by definition the pursuit of flesh of the same kind. Whether the men of Sodom knew these were angels is of little consequence, however. Jude 7 clearly puts sexual immorality in Sodom and says, "They serve as an example of those who suffer the punishment of eternal fire."

Jesus indicated in Luke 10:14 that those of this generation who rejected the rule of God would receive a harsher judgment than those

---

[91] Richard Hayes, <u>Moral Vision of the New Testament</u> (San Francisco, Harper Collins Publishers, 1996), pg. 405.

at Sodom and Gomorrah. Unbelief – refusal to receive God's rule over and in our lives, from Genesis to Jesus – is THE SIN; all else flows from this DISASTER! This is why Jesus speaks harshly here. Also, in the person of Jesus, an unprecedented opportunity for deliverance came to Israel but was in large part rejected. This multiplied the crisis and the DISASTER of unbelief, a disaster even greater than Sodom!

LEVITICUS

The book of Leviticus is dominated by one admonition, "Be holy as I am Holy." (Lev. 11:44). Leviticus 18:22 and 20:13, a part of several chapters in Leviticus described as the Holiness Code, explicitly prohibits male homosexual intercourse. "You shall not lie with a male as with a woman; it is an abomination." (Lev. 18:22) In Leviticus 20:13, the same act is listed as one of a series of sexual offenses – along with adultery, incest, and bestiality – that are punishable by death. It is worth noting that the act of "lying with a male as with a woman" is categorically forbidden; *motives* for the act are not treated as a morally significant factor. This passage was the foundation for the universal rejection of male same-sex intercourse within Judaism.

Even Derrick Bailey says that the Holiness Code understood these acts to violate the order of creation. The term "abomination", he notes, "is closely associated with idolatry, and designates not only false gods, but also the worship and conduct of those who serve them. By a natural extension of meaning, however, it can also be whatever reverses the proper order of things, and this seems to be the connotation of *to'ebah* (abomination) as applied to homosexual acts in Leviticus. Such acts are regarded as 'abomination', not … because they were practiced by Egyptian or Canaanite idolaters (for of this there is no proof), but because, as a reversal of what is sexually natural, they exemplify the spirit of idolatry which is itself the fundamental subversion of true order."[92]

---

[92] Derrick Bailey, Homosexuality and the Western Christian Tradition, (New York: Longmans, Green and Co., 1955), pg. 68.

In other words, these acts violate the created order of male and female and are *to'ebah* (abomination); they are an idolatrous affront to the integrity of the deity.

Clearly, the Holiness Code regarding sexuality, adultery, incest, and homosexual acts is in basic principle committed to the defense of family and married life, and everything outside family and married life is seen as a threat and an outrage, an abomination not to be permitted in Israel.[93] Read the entire context of Leviticus 18-20 for the moral concerns of the writer.

Letha Scanzoni, an avowed evangelical Christian, argues in her book, Is the Homosexual My Neighbor?, that the three reasons for Israel's Holiness Code are as follows:

(1) Separation from the customs of other nations
(2) Avoidance of idolatry
(3) Ceremonial uncleanness

Scanzoni argues that these issues in Leviticus no longer are important for the church. She then goes on to ask "If the Israelite Holiness Code is to be invoked against 20th century homosexuals, it should likewise be invoked against such practices as eating rare steak … and having marital intercourse during the menstrual period."[94]

In other words, why single out the moral laws and not the dietary and ceremonial ones? The answer is fairly simple: "Because Jesus and Paul, as his follower, did." Scanzoni ignores the distinctions made by both Paul and Jesus. Jesus obliterated the food laws but deepened the prohibition against adultery (Matt. 5:17-48; Mark 7:6-23); Paul did the same in Romans 14:13-17 and I Cor. 6:9-20. Even a superficial reading of Leviticus 18 reveals the Lord God declaring punishment for child sacrifice (20:1ff) and commanding generosity to the needy (19:9-10) as well as forbidding incest and adultery

---

[93] Stanley Grenz, Welcoming But Not Affirming, (Louisville, Kentucky, Westminster John Knox Press, 1998), pg. 46.

[94] Letha Scanzoni and Virginia Ramey Mollenkott, Is the Homosexual My Neighbor? Another Christian View (San Francisco, Harper and Row, 1978), pg. 59-61.

(chapters 18-20). Neither Jesus nor his followers abolished these moral, non-ceremonial laws.

The argument continues to be made that the homosexuality in Leviticus is an abomination, not because it is inherently evil but because the Gentiles did it, and were therefore ritually impure.[95] Therefore, these laws have no relevance for today's Church. Such arguments ignore the text of Leviticus 18-20 and the clear teachings of Jesus and Paul who made distinctions between ceremonial and moral laws. This argument presumes to know too much about Leviticus and refuses to learn anything from Jesus, who clearly abandoned the Jewish food laws while calling his disciples to a higher standard of inside-out sexual morality. (Matt. 5:17-48; Mark 7:6-23)

Gomes' argument that the ritual purity concerns of the Levitical laws have no relevance to today's church simply ignores the clear teaching of Jesus and Paul as to the authority of these laws for today. We must look at the entire canon of Scripture, allowing all of the texts, Old Testament and New, to speak to us.

Did first-generation Christianity consider the prohibition of same-sex acts, adultery or incest as forbidden in Leviticus an obsolete standard of holiness? The answer is no! In 1 Corinthians 5:1-6:20, Paul addresses incest, homosexual sin and adultery issues as profoundly moral and spiritual issues.

1 CORINTHIANS 5:6-20

The early church did in fact consistently adopt the Old Testament's teaching on matters of sexual morality, including homosexual acts. Yet Paul's overriding concern in the immediate context of 1 Corinthians 5:11 and 6:11, where homosexual sins are mentioned, is the "failure of the church to be the church." In 5:1-5, he expresses his outrage at the case of incest within the church. The Corinthians are failing to act as a community, failing to take responsibility for one another, failing to discipline the man in incest and failing to take responsibility for settling their own disputes, thus suing each

---

[95] Peter Gomes, The Good Book (New York, Willard Morrow and Company, 1996), pg. 154.

other in pagan courts. In behaving this way, they declare primary allegiances to the pagan culture rather than the community of faith.

Paul's argument highlights the tragic contrast between the church's glorious last days destiny and its present failure to exercise jurisdiction over her disputes. Their behavior is completely inconsistent with their new identity in Christ.[96]

It is then that Paul fills in the content of the general term "wrongdoer" by giving a list of types of people who will not inherit the Kingdom. "But now I am writing to you that you must not associate with anyone who calls himself a brother but is sexually immoral (*pornos*), or greedy, an idolater or a slanderer, a drunkard or a swindler. With such a man do not even eat." (1 Cor. 5:11) Whereas the Old Testament practices the death penalty in punishment for these offenses, the new covenant Scriptures withdraw a practical, real fellowship.

One chapter later, after discussing the issues of believers suing one another in pagan law courts, Paul concludes, "Instead you yourselves cheat and do wrong and you do this to your brothers."(6:8) This behavior is utterly inconsistent with who we are and whose we are. It should not be tolerated in the church. He goes on to say, "Do you not know that the wicked will not inherit the Kingdom of God? Do not be deceived. Neither the sexually immoral (*pornos*) nor idolaters, nor adulterers (*moikoi*), nor male prostitutes (*malakoi*) nor homosexual offenders (*arsenokoitai*) nor thieves, nor the greedy, nor the drunkards, nor slanderers, nor swindlers will inherit the Kingdom of God. *And this is what some of you were.* But you were washed, you were sanctified, you were justified in the name of our Lord Jesus Christ and by the Spirit of God." (6:11)

This passage (6:11) repeats the sin offenses listed in 5:11 and adds four more: adulterers, thieves, male prostitutes and homosexual offenders. It is not surprising that Paul would link these four, including the same-sex sins with the other items in his previous list (5:11), all which also, according to the Old Testament, required the offender to be executed.

---

[96] The discussion of 1 Corinthians 5:6-20 is shaped in part by my reading of Hayes, op. cit. at pgs. 390-394.

This entire context, 5:1-6:11, is not fundamentally about homosexuality. Same-sex sins are listed along with eight other sins as having no place in the Kingdom of God. The immediate context contains these overriding concerns: (1) The church must act as a responsible counter-culture, reflecting the Last Days reality. It is significant to note that in 6:7-8, Paul says it is better to suffer for being wronged rather than to do wrong. *Do not expect the Christian life to give you fulfillment now!* We live in the tension between the now and the not yet of the Kingdom of God. We do not expect or dream of fulfillment in this life! We dream of fulfillment in the coming consummated Kingdom of God. This has enormous implications for the legally wronged, the divorced, the homosexual and for every one of us!

In 6:1-8, legal disputes between Christians jeopardize the unity of the church and completely obliterates her witness as an alternative parallel society to a pagan world. The Corinthians are to stop "seeing" themselves as participants in the normal social and economic structures of their city and to imagine themselves instead as members of the last days people of God, acting corporately in a way that will prefigure and proclaim the Kingdom of God.[97]

This entire context in Corinthians is almost completely ignored by today's church. But it is within this context that Paul begins listing behaviors that do not belong within the Kingdom of God. Included within this list are two words descriptive of homosexual sin. The term translated male prostitute (*malakoi*) is not a technical term for homosexuality; no such term existed in Greek or Hebrew at the time. It does appear often in Hellenistic Greek as slang to describe the passive partners, often young boys, in homosexual activity. The second word, *arsenokotai*, translated homosexual offenders in the NIV is not found in any current Greek texts of the time. It appears that the word *arsenokotai* is a translation of the Hebrew *mishlcay zakur* (lying with a male) derived from Lev. 18:22 and 20:13 and used in rabbinic texts to refer to homosexual intercourse.[98] Paul is

---

[97]-Ibid., p.98

[98]-Ibid., p. 382

using the same Greek word in 1 Cor. 6:11 as was used in the Greek translation of Lev. 18 and 20 to refer to homosexual intercourse.

The Greek Old Testament translation (The Septuagint) of Leviticus 20:13 reads, "Whoever lies with a man as with a woman (*meta arsenos koiten gunaikos*), they have both done an abomination." Thus, Paul's use of the term presupposes and reaffirms the Holiness Code's condemnation of homosexual acts.

But Paul goes on to say in reference to the list of wrongdoing, "And that is what some of you were. But you were washed, you were sanctified, you were justified in the name of the Lord Jesus Christ and by the Spirit of our God" (6:11). I Corinthians 6:11 does not single out homosexual acts among the list of wrongdoing. All of the wrongdoers have been forgiven of past sins (washed), set apart for God's purposes (sanctified) and placed in right relation to God in the community of God's people (justified). The notion that those who struggle with same-sex sins bear a shame or should be ostracized has no basis in the Scripture. Jesus liberates and gives new identity! Paul always lists same-sex sins as "matter-of-factly" as he lists all other sins.

In the context immediately following this one, Paul argues against the frequenting of temple prostitutes by the Corinthian men (1 Cor. 6:12-20). The sexual latitude allowed to men by Greek public opinion was virtually unrestricted. Sexual relations of males with both boys and harlots were generally tolerated. In Corinthians 6:12-20, Paul argues that our body belongs to the Lord and that the sexual acts of the body possess significance beyond the mere eating of food. Paul, on the basis of our relationship to Christ, contends that fornication has no place in the believer's life. He concludes, "Do you not know that your body is a temple of the Holy Spirit, who is in you, whom you have received from God? You are not your own; you were bought at a price. Therefore, honor God with your body" (6:19-20). Do temple worship in your body at all times! This goes for all of us whatever our sexual preferences may be.

There are those who claim that the dominant expression of same-sex love in the Greco-Roman world was pederasty (sex between an adult male and an adolescent boy) but Paul nowhere appears to be condemning homosexuality primarily on the grounds that it was an exploitative mismatch, but on the grounds that homosexual acts are a willful chosen rejection of God's design for sexuality (See Romans 1:18-32).

Plato's Symposium contained moving statements about the compassionate and beautiful character of same-sex love, describing various celebrants (including Socrates) during a time of light drinking after a banquet that occurred in 416 B.C. [99] Plutarch's Dialogues (750 B.C.) contained strong affirmation of loving same-sex relationships, contending for their superiority over heterosexual lovemaking. The same attitude was defended in the Pseudo-Lucianic Affairs of the Heart (ca. 300 A.D.). These references indicate that the ancient context contained powerful proponents of adult same-sex lovemaking not unlike the contemporary context of the early 21st century.

Then, as now, pagan writers advocated exploitative homosexual acts as well as homosexual acts of love. It is the lack of gender polarity, thereby distorting God's created intent, that is at the root of the Biblical as well as the contemporary church's opposition to homosexuality. (Romans 1:18-32, Genesis 1 and 2)

1 TIMOTHY 1:10

1 Timothy 1:10 includes *arsenokotai* (homosexual offenders) in the list of "the lawless and disobedient," whose behavior is specified in a vice list that includes everything from lying to slave trading, to murdering one's parents, under the overview of actions "contrary to the sound teaching that conforms to the glorious gospel." Here again the Old Testament prohibition is presupposed, but the context offers little discussion of sexual morality as such.

ROMANS 1:18-32

Romans 1:18-32 describes the unrighteousness of fallen humanity. Man refuses to honor God and the wrath of God is revealed against all ungodliness and wickedness of those who suppress the

---

[99] Robert Gagnon The Bible and Homosexual Practice (Nashville, Abingdon Press, 2001), p. 351.

truth (1:18). "God gave them up" occurs three times (1:24,26,28). The wrath of God "gave them up" to sexual impurity, etc. Moral sin is the result of God's wrath, not the <u>reason</u> for it. We "act out" immorally because God's judgment gives us up to get what we want. Ignorance is the consequence of humanity's primal rebellion. We suppress moral truth; we don't know or want to know what we know.

"God gave them over in the sinful desires of their hearts to sexual impurity" (1:26). These various forms of the "debased mind" and "things that should not be done" are seen to be <u>manifestations</u> of God's wrath. Paul is not warning his readers that they will incur the wrath of God if they do the things he lists. Rather, he is describing rampant lawlessness as evidence that God's wrath and judgment are <u>already</u> at work in the world. Secondly, these depravities demonstrate man's otherwise hidden "ungodliness and wickedness."

Paul's portrayal of homosexual behavior is of an illustrative character; but it is obviously ungodly for Paul in that it flouts sexual distinctions that are fundamental to God's creative design in Genesis 1 and 2. "When human beings engage in homosexual activity, they enact an outward and visible sign of an inward and spiritual reality.[100] That reality is sin!

The exchange of the glory of God for idols (1:23) leads to a tragic rebellious trade-off: "Their women exchanged natural relations for unnatural and the men likewise gave up natural relations with women and were consumed with passion for one another" (1:26-27). For Paul, nature refers to the created order, not what actually exists in every man but what ought to be, of the world as designed by God and revealed through the stories and laws of Scripture.

The Jewish community as well as the Greco-Roman philosophy of Jesus' time appealed to nature in their arguments against the homosexual practices of their era.[101] Josephus, the foremost Jewish historian of the period, says, "The Law recognizes no sexual connections except for the natural union of man and wife ... But it abhors

---

[100]-Ibid., p. 386

[101]-Ibid., p.405.

the intercourse of males with males and punishes any who undertake such a thing with death."[102]

The following are noteworthy observations from Romans 1:24-31: (1) Paul is giving a global view of the universal fall, not a description of individual life histories. (2) Homosexual intercourse is mentioned because it is one embodiment of the spiritual condition of those who have "exchanged the truth about God for a lie." (3) Homosexual acts are not, however, especially reprehensible sins. They are no worse in principle than covetousness, gossip or disrespect for parents. (4) Homosexual activity is its own reward, an "anti-reward" reflecting God's wrath – his "giving us up" as a result of our idolatry. Preoccupation with sex was a sign of a world in spiritual rebellion and disarray! It still is!

Paul treats all homosexual activity as well as all heterosexual activity outside marriage as credible evidence of humanity's tragic confusion and alienation from God the Creator. For Paul all homosexual acts result not from over-sexed heterosexuals but from man's rebellion against God leading to sexual acts in opposition to the created order of the sexes (Romans 1:18-32). Sex becomes a new creaturely idol.

Some argue that the Bible has no category for homosexuals with an exclusively same-sex orientation and that same-sex passion was thought to originate in over-sexed heterosexuals. But Paul never said that same-sex acts originated in over-sexed heterosexuals, nor did the pagan culture of Paul's day understand same-sex acts and/or orientation to result from over-sexed heterosexuals. The fact is that the notion of the innateness of homosexual passion in some persons at the time of Paul existed in the myth of human origins expounded in Plato's Symposium (5th Century BC) and other influential ancient texts, including the writings of Aristotle (4th century BC) and later Philostratus (3rd century A.D.).[103] The ancient pagan cultural context with its myths of homosexual innateness is not all that much unlike the contemporary 21st century context with its arguments for the innateness and beauty of consenting adult homosexual passion.

---

[102] Josephus, **Against Apion**, p. 199, cited in Ibid, p.170-171.

[103] Gagnon, op.cit., p.384

Paul's attitude toward the person who <u>felt</u> gay, but did not desire it would be one of fellowship, but not one which allowed for homosexual acts. Paul would consider such an "orientation" as subject to change within the Body of Christ and in the power of the Spirit. This is the only conclusion consistent with Paul's statements in Romans 1 and 1 Corinthians 6:11.

Romans 1 and 2 should transform the tone and the terms of our contemporary debate about homosexuality: the screamers, whether on the side of gay rights or on the side of gay bashing, have no place. All of us are flattened by a humbling God who declares that every last one of us is in need of God's mercy. First, worship God. Then, while on your knees, pray for humility. Then, get into your chairs and turn towards those with whom you disagree, ready to pray for them, listen to them and speak the truth in love to them.

It is important to note that Romans 1:18-32 sets up a spiritual trap door for the self-righteous believer. The anti-gay homophobics of the church then and now read Romans 1:18-32 with frenzied indignation but stop short of Romans 2:1: "Therefore, you have no excuse, whoever you are, when you judge others, for in passing judgment on another, you condemn yourself because you, the judge, are doing the very same things." The overall point of Romans 1-3 is simply this: None are righteous, no not one. ALL have sinned – homosexual, heterosexual, gossiper, liars, Jews or Gentiles – and fallen short of the glory of God (Romans 3). A self-righteous judgment of homosexuality is just as sinful as the homosexual behavior itself! We must make *moral judgments*, but we never judge others with a self-righteous pious arrogance. *Never!*

DISCUSSION QUESTIONS

1. What do the Old Testament Scriptures say is the "sin of Sodom"?
2. Do you think the prohibitions against homosexuality in Lev. 18-20 are authoritative for today's church? Why or why not?
3. What about Scanzoni's argument?

4. Discuss homosexual sin as it is referred to in 1 Corinthians 5:1-6:11.
5. Homosexual sin is the result of the judgment of God, not the cause of it in Romans 1:18-32. Discuss.
6. Do you see any affirmed homosexual relationships in Scripture?
7. Discuss the relevance of the ancient pagan views of homosexuality. What did Plato think of homosexuality?

Homosexuality within the Bible's Theology

❧❦❧

"The old scriptures include commands prohibiting homosexuality, but so what? I know that if I <u>love</u> another person that whatever we consent to do together as an expression of our love <u>cannot</u> be wrong in the sight of Jesus. By the way, Jesus never spoke out against homosexuality."

"I can love the Father, Son and Spirit and claim the blood of Jesus for my sins, but I don't have to accept what the Scripture says about homosexuality."

But is it so easy? What if the Biblical teachings on sexual ethics are intimately knitted together with Biblical notions of Creation, Sin, New Creation and the return of Christ? All of us try to wiggle out at this point – heterosexual and homosexual alike! All of us want to pick and choose what we obey.

Lets examine the theology of the Bible and the actual <u>contexts</u> where homosexuality is mentioned. Hopefully we will stop our <u>pre-texting</u> and <u>proof-texting</u>!

No consideration of homosexuality can rest content with a short list of passages that treat the matter explicitly. We have lined up scriptures, removed from their context, to argue for the righteousness of slavery and the subjugation of woman. This approach always removes the specific passage at issue from the great themes of Scripture. The context of the passage is lost and when the context is lost the scripture can be used against itself.

We must consider how the scripture frames the issue more broadly. What is the theology of the Bible within which homosexuality is referenced? What is our working theology as we read the scriptures?

Though only a few biblical texts speak of homoerotic behavior, all that do mention it express unqualified disapproval. In this respect, the issue of homosexuality differs significantly from matters such as slavery, war or the subordination of woman, in which the Bible contains internal tensions and counterpoised witnesses. The biblical witness against homosexual practices is unanimous in Old and New Testaments. The contexts in which homosexuality is mentioned differ, but the conclusion is the same. The theological contexts for the Bible's conclusions regarding homosexuality include the following: the Biblical doctrine of created man-woman sexual polarity (Genesis 1 and 2, Matthew 19:1-9), the Leviticus Holiness Code with it's overriding concern for the set-apartness of God's people (Leviticus 18-20), and the notions of sin and liberation from sin (Romans 1:18-32 and 1 Corinthians 6:1-11).

Consider first the theology of God's creative intention for human sexuality. From Genesis 1 onward, scripture repeatedly affirms that God has made man and woman for one another and that our sexual desires rightly find their fulfillment within heterosexual marriage (Genesis 1 and 2, Mark 10:2-9, Matt. 19:1-12, 1 Thess. 4:3-8, 1 Cor. 7:1-9, Eph. 5:21-33, Heb. 13:4). The Song of Solomon celebrates unashamedly the male and female bodies in poetic celebration of marital lovemaking. The biblical view of sexuality does not depend on a list of forbidden activities but on the pervasiveness and reasonableness of an affirmed activity within God's created order – heterosexual marriage. The Bible sees the polarity of the sexes uniting in one flesh, the producing and rearing of children and the responsibility of both covenant married partners to one another and their children as the foundational elements of marriage.[104]

Next, examine the fallen human condition. The Bible offers an account of human bondage to sin (Gen. 3-11, Rom. 1:18-32). As great grandchildren of a Jeffersonian enlightenment, we like to think

---

[104] Thomas Schmidt, Straight and Narrow. (Downers Grove, Illinois, Intervarsity Press, 1995), p.51

of ourselves as free moral agents, choosing rationally among possible actions. But scripture unmasks this cheerful illusion and teaches us that we are deeply infected by the tendency to self-deception! Do we take Jefferson, Franklin and Emerson's optimistic assessment of man as a "good rational animal"? Or do we take Jeremiah, Paul and Jesus' assessment of man as a corrupted enslaved child of God? (Jer. 17:9; Rom. 1:21-22, 32, 6:17) We opt for Jesus. We are "slaves of sin" apart from Christ. Redemption means "being emancipated from slavery."

The very nature of sin is that it is not always freely chosen. It is not true biblically that only freely-chosen acts are morally culpable. In the light of this biblical view of man and sin, it cannot be maintained that a homosexual orientation is morally neutral because it is or becomes involuntary. Neither can it be said that an alcoholic or rage-aholic orientation is morally neutral because it is or becomes involuntary.[105] No research has shown that a homosexual act or orientation is an involuntary state. But it should be admitted that what begins as a choice often becomes a bondage.

I have an attorney friend who has been married several times. He has decided that he is just not "wired" for monogamy. He recently divorced his fifth wife and is now "dating" permanently. His relationship to the Lord Jesus, if it exists, has no stated, discernible impact on his ability to be married. He has no relationship with the body of Christ. He "loves" people, especially women. He is conventionally very nice and is a reasonably good father. In his case, "whatever is" is good. He believes we live in a non-judgmental, right to privacy, relativistic culture.

Needless to say, my friend's approach to "whatever is" ignores the biblical notion of sin and the notion that anybody needs liberating. I deny that God made my friend this way. He may have had a propensity to "befriend" women at birth but his history suggests that he learned this behavior. Seeking to understand my friend and myself in the light of Christ and his scripture, and not according to my opinion, is of singular importance here. As I understand him I understand myself!

---

[105] Richard Hayes, op. cit., p. 390

Many of the advocates of no-fault divorce, open marriages, and unqualified acceptance of homosexuality seem to be operating with a simplistic anthropology that assumes that "whatever is" must be good. They have a theology of creation but no theology of sin and redemption. Yet the biblical writers would understand Bill's "wiring" as sin, whether it is inherited, volitional or both. Throughout Scripture, the notion of sin's willfulness is also accompanied by the notion of bondage. Bondage indicates the loss of choice. This is where all sins are headed!

The Bible clearly describes a fallen biology, psychology and sociology. Not one of us came onto a perfect earth with untainted DNA. We are born into a fallen world by fallen parents. Our nine-month passage through our Mother's womb is now a dangerous season, threatened by disease, drugs, abortion and violence. The dangers, threats and fallenness continue with us from birth!

Yet the notion of sin in our time has been replaced by the language of therapy. Phillip Reiff's classic book, <u>The Triumph of the Therapeutic</u>, discusses the victory of therapeutic language and concepts over biblical language and concepts. We are obsessed with the self, not with the soul. Most mothers in the U.S.A. prioritize for their children a good self-concept above their child's following Jesus. The Godly mother, biblically speaking, was passionately concerned with the holiness of her child for God (i.e. the child's set apartness for God). Self-actualization as now understood in our therapeutic culture not a biblical concept.

The language of the therapeutic now supports the notion that sin has little if any relevance for modern people and exalts the goodness of "whatever is" as long as the "whatever is" does not inflict tissue damage on another human being. This is the optimism of Thomas Jefferson and contemporary non-directive, non-judgmental psychology mixed, mingled and popularized. When disciples of Jesus grapple with moral issues, we must take the biblical notions of sin seriously while seeking to discern the will of God, our culture's notions not withstanding.

Thirdly, consider the theology of the Bible's witness to the reality of a present liberation in Christ, not yet fully realized and how that concept undercuts our cultural obsession with sexual fulfillment, sexual images and sexual sins. Scripture and history itself bear witness that lives of freedom, joy and service are possible without sexual relations. Matthew 19:10-12 and 1 Corinthians 7:32-35 clearly commend the celibate way of life as a way of faithfulness. Sexual activity within scripture never becomes the basis for defining a person's identity or for finding meaning and fulfillment in life. Sexual fulfillments find their place, at best, as a subsidiary good within the larger picture of a restored friendship with God. The larger command is "Honor God with your body" (1 Cor. 6:20). Within that directive we discover what God wants of each one of us.

THE CENTRALITY OF THE CHRIST

It is crucial that we probe the significance of Jesus the Anointed One, resurrected Lord, for the life of the Church! Everything is changed by the coming of Christ, his incarnation, his life, death and resurrection. "God was in Christ reconciling the world to himself, not counting their trespasses against them, and entrusting the message of reconciliation to us." (2 Cor. 5:19) Jesus is Lord! He stands as Lord of the Old Testament, speaking in ways that ratify, modify and judge Old Testament teachings.

Jesus never addressed the issue of homosexuality. Jesus' silence, however, is no argument pro or con. Jesus did announce the rule of God (Kingdom), he promised to pour out the Holy Spirit, and he spoke of dying for us and rising on the third day. Jesus clearly embraced the great texts of the Old Testament (e.g. Gen 1 and 2) calling Israel to faithful heterosexual monogamy (Matt. 19:1-9; Mark 10:1-9). The character of Jesus and his resurrection presence among us causes us to prayerfully consider all that we do in the light of his overpowering presence among us. (1 Cor. 6:12-20).

CROSS OF CHRIST

When scriptures speak of ethical concerns, it is done in the context of Christ's cross, of Christ's community and the new creation in Christ. The cross of Christ is the glory of the New Testament. Wrath is not the last word. Human rebellion creates the condition of crisis that makes the death of Jesus necessary (Rom. 5:8). Romans 8:3-4 indicates that Christ's death as a sin offering and the Holy Spirit within us makes possible "the just requirement of the law being fulfilled in us"(Rom. 8:3-4).

The cross models the way the church ought to respond to those of homosexual inclinations – not in rejection but in sacrificial service! This is especially true in light of the AIDS epidemic. It is also of enormous significance for a church that knows more about how to shame those who struggle with same-sex sins than it knows about nurturing and releasing the Lord's presence in and forgiveness to them. Furthermore, the cross marks the end of the old life under the power of sin and the beginning of a new life baptized into Christ (Rom. 6:1-4). No one in Christ is locked into the past or into a psychological or biological determinism. The judgment of Romans 1 should never be read apart from the rest of the letter with its message of Grace, Hope and Power through Christ's cross (Romans 5-8).

COMMUNITY OF CHRIST

The biblical prohibitions against homosexual behavior are concerned not just for the private morality of individuals but for the health, wholeness and purity of the elect community. This is evident in the Holiness Code of Leviticus 18:6-26 and 1 Corinthians 5:1-6:20. The New Testament never considers sexual conduct a matter of purely private concern between consenting adults. According to Paul, everything that we do as Christians, including our sexual practices, affects the whole body of Christ. This is the logic behind his demand that the Corinthian church expel the man engaged in a sexual relationship with his stepmother (1 Cor. 5:1-13). A similar logic would certainly apply within Paul's frame of reference to the *malakoi* (male prostitutes) and *arsenokotai* (homosexual offenders) of 1 Corinthians 6:11. Those who act in rebellion against God are subject to discipline. The church also provides *koinonia* within which living out the obedience of faith is supported and sustained.

The significance of *koinonia* (sharing) for those struggling and sometimes failing with same-sex sins has not been understood by today's church. The church "banishes" same-sex struggles to para-church organizations and psychotherapists. Yet the church, her healthy, spiritual and physical relationships, are God's primary means for redeeming homosexuals and heterosexuals. This is of great importance for Paul, for example, as he admonishes the Corinthians, Romans and Galatians to be a "Redeeming Community" together in which all are being made holy (1 Cor. 6:11).

NEW CREATION IN CHRIST

Neither the word of judgment against homosexuality nor the hope of transformation should be read apart from the end-times framework. The Christian community lives in a time of tension between the "already" and "not yet." Already we have the joy of the Holy Spirit, but we do not yet experience the fullness of redemption. This means Christians set free from the power of sin through Christ's death must continue to struggle to live faithfully in the present time. Those who demand fulfillment now, as though it were a right or guarantee, are living in a state of adolescent illusion. Consequently, in this time between the times, some may find disciplined abstinence the only viable alternative to disordered sexuality.[106] Yet it is also true that the "now" of the Holy Spirit in us, the forgiveness of God on us and the New Community around us will give many the power to change. Does not the declaration of 1 Corinthians 6:11 "For such were some of you" declare the present redemptive power of the Now in the church? Yes. A thousand times – YES!

The biblical portrayal of human beings as fallen creatures in bondage to sin and yet set free in Christ for obedience suggests a different assessment of the meanings, purposes and importance of our sexuality. This assessment looks to the future resurrection as the place of bodily fulfillment in a New Heaven and a New Earth.

New Testament end-times, by definition, is living in the tension of the Now and the Not Yet, undergoing its frustration and fulfillment, brokenness and healing (Rom. 8:18-23). The notion of biblical end-times Christianity divides us from our permissive Revisionist

---

[106] IBID

brothers. The permissive Revisionists have omitted the Not Yet, expecting, even <u>demanding</u>, personal fulfillment with "sexual" salvation now! This approach lords sexual fulfillment, not only over scripture, but over Jesus the Lord! John McNeil, a Roman Catholic theologian and psychotherapist acknowledges his sexual agenda when approaching scripture:

"We lesbian and gay believers have the right and the duty to carefully scrutinize all religious belief systems and distinguish between those belief systems that <u>support</u> our need to achieve healthy self-acceptance and those that are <u>destructive</u> of our psychic health and maturity."[107]

The Now and the Not Yet of the Last Days promises no one absolute fulfillment, including sexual fulfillment now. McNeil is demanding a New Earth now, a place where he can sexually self-actualize, as he understands it. Heterosexuals demand no less when we dump our wives for a more self-fulfilling woman, demanding the New Earth now, a place where we can sexually self-actualize, as we understand it. We cannot bless the heterosexual's destructive agenda while disciplining those in bondage to a homosexual agenda. The claims of Christ on our bodies demand that we treat all sexual immorality with Godly evenhandedness.

Given the unanimity of the scripture's witness regarding homosexuality and the reasons for the fundamental opposition to homosexuality in the Bible, the Bible's teaching on homosexuality cannot be dismissed by a wave of the hand. The clear intent of Jesus to empower his disciples to live out the Creator's intention for a <u>man</u> and a <u>woman</u> in marriage (Matt. 19:1-9), the description of homosexual acts as well as adultery as a sign of man's sinful rebellion (Rom. 1:18-32) and the declaration in 1 Corinthians 6:11 that "such were some of you" referring to the transformation of homosexuals, adulterers, etc., <u>integrate</u> the biblical teaching on homosexuality within the <u>fundamental</u> theology of the Bible. When we ignore the biblical argument on homosexuality we must also throw away the biblical doctrines of Creation, Sin and New Creation. We must also throw away the Biblical theology of the Community of God.

---

[107] John McNeill <u>Taking a Chance on God</u> (Boston, Beacon Press, 1996), p. 21

People get redeemed from sin whether its racism, pornography or homosexuality, within community. Paul is declaring such in 1 Corinthians 6:11. If all sin is now to be reinterpreted according to opinions and human experiences so that we can all "feel good about ourselves," there is no need whatsoever for the redeeming community of broken believers who must live in the tension of Salvation and Sin! This tension calls all of us to repent, confess and believe everyday. "When a brother is overtaken in sin, you who have the Spirit restore such a one." (Galatians 6:1,2) This is the ongoing work of the church. But the need for powerful counter-cultural community is rendered obsolete when we gut the biblical view of homosexuality, divorce or gluttony as sin.

DO THE LOVING THING?

There are numerous Christian believers who no longer adhere to the basic theology of the Bible as discussed above. They rather do a revisionist gutting of the biblical theology, only to leave standing the doctrine of love. For these people the word love is the primary theological image through which to bring the New Testament text into clear perspective. The argument is simply "Jesus said to love each other. If two same-sex people truly love each other their marriage cannot be in opposition to the will of God."

This argument of "love", upon first hearing it, tends to seduce the untutored. But the wiser realize that Jesus said much more than "Love each other." Jesus' embodiment of love was more significant and instructive than what he said about love. He clearly taught us to love, but Jesus' primary message was "God rules." Jesus proclaimed a radically reinterpreted and reenvisioned Kingdom of God (See the four Gospels). It is impossible to reduce (1) Jesus' concern that heterosexual marriage be lived out in harmony with God's creative intentions (Matt. 19:1-9; Mark 10:1-10), (2) Jesus' commandments as reflective of God's will (Matt. 5-7), and (3) the reality of the Holy Spirit's life in my body leading me to sexual holiness (1 Cor. 6:11-20) to one question: "Can two homosexuals love each other?" Paul in 1 Cor. 5:1ff when he tells the Corinthian church to discipline the man living in an incestual relationship does not even ask whether the man <u>loved</u> his Father's wife with whom he was having sex. The question was <u>irrelevant</u>. The man was violating the Lord's intentions for his creation within marriage.

In Romans 13:8-10 Paul says that love <u>summarizes</u> the law, referencing commands "Do not commit adultery", "Do not covet", "Do not murder", and "Do not steal". Paul never said that love is a <u>substitute</u> for law. Neither Jesus nor Paul would dream of saying, "If you love your sexual partner adultery or homosexual intercourse is permitted."

Love is part of a much larger theological-ethical reality. Love is given direction by commandment, God's created order, Community, Holy Spirit, the Cross of Christ and by the Now and Not Yet tension of the End Times.

It is here that we must be careful. When reading a pro-gay marriage book by a Christian theologian such as Daniel A. Helminiak's <u>What the Bible Really Says About Homosexuality</u>, ask yourself, "What does this man believe?" For example, hidden away in his introduction is the following: "I do not presume the Bible provides the last word on sexual ethics."[108] If it doesn't, who or what does? He never says. At the end of the book he gives his "big view" statement of Christian ethics:

> "If they [lesbians and gay men] rely on the Bible for guidance and inspiration, lesbians and gay men will certainly feel bound by the core moral teachings of the Judeo-Christian tradition: be prayerful, reverence God, respect others, be loving and kind, be forgiving and merciful, be honest and be just. Work for harmony and peace. Stand up for truth. Give of yourself for all that is good, and avoid all that you know to be evil. To do that is to follow God's way. To do that is to love God with your whole heart and soul. To do that is to be a true disciple of Jesus."[109]

---

[108] Joseph Helminiak, <u>What the Bible Really Says About Homosexuality</u>, San Francisco, Alamo Press, 1995), p. 13.

[109]-<u>Ibid</u>., p. 108

I find this paragraph at first blush to be very compelling. I don't doubt the writer's sincerity. He reflects a widespread notion that Jesus primarily said, "Love each other." Yet Jesus said much more than "Love each other." For example, Jesus announced the Kingdom of God many times, manifested an enormous respect for righteousness, calling his disciples to a greater righteousness than the law, and spoke of heterosexual monogamy as God's norm for all time (See Mark 10; Matt. 19:1-9).

Helminiak's statement of ethics, however innocent it may appear, allows for adultery, bestiality, polygamy, etc. as long as it is done with love and respect! It would also allow for living with your opposite or same-sex lover as long as you treat one another with respect, kindness and love. Helminiak's read on scripture never refers to his theological convictions as to the order of creation, sin, the death of Christ, the power of the Holy Spirit, the inspiration and authority of scripture, the church, or the end-times. Helminiak says that fundamental mistake at the heart of the homosexual debate "must be in how the Bible is read."[110] I disagree. The homosexual "debate" reveals sin within the "*gay*" and "*straight*" communities and great differences among Christians as to the basic theology of the Bible.

Helminiak does some exegetical work in his book, leaning heavily on scholars such as John Boswell, William L. Countryman and Robin Scraggs, all advocates of homosexual marriage. His overriding theology purports to show that all of the statements in scripture against homosexuality can be dismissed as irrelevant for one reason or another.

Helminiak strains to interpret the Greek words malakai (male prostitute) and arsenokotai (homosexual offender) as referring to unloving, disrespectful homosexual acts. Therefore, these words are not applicable to a "loving, respectful" homosexual relationship today. Yet who is to say that the first-century homosexual behavior referenced in 1 Corinthians 6:11 or Romans 1:18-32 was not "loving and respectful?" Helminiak's strained exegesis and application for today blunts the sharp edges of the word of God.

---

[110]-Ibid., p. 26

He finally concludes, "So the Bible takes no direct stand on the morality of homogenital acts as such nor on the morality of gay and lesbian relationships."[111] If this is true, then the Bible takes no stand on thievery, gossip, greed, jealousy, adultery, murder, etc.! For the same contexts that speak of same-sex sins speak of thievery, gossip, greed and the like (See 1 Cor. 6:1-20, Rom. 1:18-32).

Helminiak's use of scripture reminds me of attempts made by other theologians, beginning a generation ago, to justify sex outside of marriage if the married partners both consented. Again, the rationale is that love for the third party and the "need" for self-actualization makes it not only morally appropriate but absolutely necessary that this adulterous relationship be pursued. The fact is that the reading of ancient as well as medieval love stories reveals that adultery is adultery is adultery! Modernized sin is no less deadly. It cannot be demonstrated that same-sex acts today are of a different quality than all those of Jesus and Paul's world.

Helminiak's book, an attempt to reduce all of biblical theology to one admonition "Do the loving thing," simply misrepresents the nature, character and richness of our lives in Christ.

DISCUSSION QUESTIONS

1. How is the Bible's view of homosexuality related to the biblical doctrine of the creation of the sexes?
2. Is a behavior morally neutral because it is involuntary? Discuss.
3. Discuss the notion "Whatever is is good."
4. How does the cross model the way we are to respond to those with homosexual inclinations?
5. Discuss the New Testament community's relationship to the same-sex struggler.
6. Should those who live in the "Now and Not Yet" of the Kingdom expect sexual fulfillment now? Discuss.
7. Discuss "If it's a loving and respectful relationship it must be godly."

---

[111]-Ibid., p. 108

Hermeneutics: Moving From Then to Now!

༺✢༻

"How in the world can you put the authority of a biblical command, principle or story above reason or human experience? How could an old book have more authority in my life today than my own informed reason? Isn't the Holy Spirit living in Christians who live in same-sex relationships? If that's true, how can the Bible's teaching possess more authority than the Holy Spirit?" I take these questions very seriously.

The issues included in moving from Scripture in the ancient world to now are legion! How can we more responsibly utilize scriptural authority in our lives? It's time to look at what we call hermeneutics – moving from what the scripture said then to what scripture means now for today's church.

Why should the scripture be accorded primacy over tradition, reason and experience in our time? A full answer is beyond the parameters of this book, but suffice it to say that the Christian affirms that God has acted in history by calling a particular people for a particular mission. The Christian view of the Incarnation asserts that truth is given to us in a particular time and place: Jesus of Nazareth. The Gospel of Jesus is not a summary of "the necessary truths of reason." Rather, he is a revelation that shatters and reshapes human reason in light of God's foolishness. The Word is known in human form, and only there. That is the scandal of the Gospel. The biblical texts authoritatively witness to the claim that God has uniquely acted in history through the seed of Abraham to redeem the world. The texts describe for us the nature of the community life that is created among us by God's act of revelation and liberation.

The early church began recognizing from the beginning in the 2nd century A.D. those books that had an authority over the church as the once-for-all apostolic witness to Jesus the Christ. This formation of a canon set these books within the Canon above the authority of church leaders and anyone else who might be tempted to write a revisionist account of the Jewish Christian faith. For about 2000 years the church has recognized this Canon Old and New Testament as her authoritative written witness, which is truly interpreted and applied only when the church humbly submits herself to the leading of God's Spirit.

Failure to acknowledge the authority of the Canon of scripture over tradition, reason and experience leads to the abandonment of basic Christian teaching regarding God, Christ, the Spirit and the nature of the Christian life. Yet it is also true that the scripture must be, in the power of the Spirit, read, interpreted and applied anew in every generation. Our methods and conclusions regarding the interpretation of scripture constitute a tradition that must be tested by each generation of believers. In every age we are admonished to handle scripture responsibly (2 Timothy 2:15) and to not be conformed to this world but transformed by the renewal of our minds so that we may see more clearly the will of God for today's Church (Romans 12:2).

It is important that we understand biblical authority to be a mediated authority, given to us and opened up to us by Jesus Christ who has all authority. In Jesus the Kingdom of God ruptures the status quo, just as new wine bursts old wineskins. Illusions of stability and authority – both the authority of Roman rule (Mark 12:13-17) and the authority of the Jewish religious establishment (Mark 11:27-12:12) – are stripped away. In Jesus the Christ, God's abrupt intervention opens up what we thought was a closed system of causes and effects and lays human life bare before God. The demons are rightly concerned that Jesus has come to destroy them! A powerful campaign against evil and sin is waged by Jesus, but unexpectedly this campaign reaches its greatest power as Jesus dies on a cross, then is astonishingly raised from the dead and a new community of believers is created by the work of the Holy Spirit on Pentecost.

We remain convinced that Jesus is alive, full of authority and power, ruling as a "slain lamb" and therefore we resist any revisionist who claims to deny, theologize or improve upon Jesus or the life of discipleship to which he calls us! The authority of the Christian scriptures resides in their unique once-for-all apostolic witness to Jesus and the life to which he calls us. Refusal to place ourselves under the authority of scripture is a refusal to place ourselves under the authority of Christ.

The original New Testament writings were written to specific churches for specific purposes. What those documents said then to the readers is the task of *exegesis*. What those documents say to the church now is the task of *hermeneutics* (interpretation). In what way are we to apply these texts to the issues that confront us now as the church faces new and forceful demands regarding the acceptance and ordination of homosexuals?

How do we apply or appropriate the handful of relevant texts on this issue? We do so by looking at the rules, principles, models and words of revelation (such as Romans 1:18-32) which reference homosexuality. First of all, it is important to note that there is no clearly articulated rule against homosexual practices in the New Testament. The Leviticus text contains a prohibition against homosexuality in rule form. Paul clearly presupposes this prohibition in Romans 1:32 and 1 Corinthians 6:9-11. Yet neither Paul nor Jesus were the teachers of new rules. The New Testament writers take the moral law of the old covenant as God's will, declaring in Romans 8 that as a result of Christ's death and the outpouring of the Spirit, the righteous requirement of the law *might be met in us* (8:4).

Secondly, although there is no clearly articulated rule against homosexuality in the New Testament, the New Testament passages in question do express ideas that can be tested as principles for governing sexual conduct. From Romans 1:21-22 we can set down the principle that human action ought to acknowledge and honor God as Creator. When read against the background of the creation story, this principle yields the conclusion that homosexuality is contrary to the will of God (Romans 1:24-27). Because we refused to praise or thank God, God gave us over to shameful lusts, including homosexual acts (vs. 26-27). This story teaches us moral truth without giving us a command. Principles flow out of stories, out of narratives. The issue is the underlying narrative. Some would say today that the controlling narrative is the plight of lesbian women and gay men throughout the world. I take seriously these narratives, but I consider a "gay" narrative or my "straight" narrative important, but not controlling. The controlling story for Christ's disciples is the story contained in the biblical revelation; it is the story of God and of all men and women, not just one slice of mankind – their creation, tragic fall, liberation by Jesus and destiny in a new Heaven and a new Earth.

1 Corinthians 6:20 says, "Glorify God with your body." This principle also flows out of the specific declarations of 6:15-19. But if the principle is removed from Christ and the relationship of our bodies to him, we can construe "Glorify God with your body" into spiritual license unrelated to Christ or scripture. I hear it said by Christians, "I never feel God's presence like I do when I make love to my girlfriend." But the principle of 1 Corinthians 6:20 leads believers to renounce the list of sins of 5:11, 6:11, and 6:12-20, however heady the feelings – no exception.

Thirdly, the only models offered by the New Testament for homosexual behavior are the emphatically negative sketches in Romans 1:18-32, 1 Corinthians 6:9 and 1 Timothy 1:10. The New Testament offers no accounts of homosexual Christians, tells no stories of same-sex lovers, and ventures no word pictures that place a positive construal on homosexual relations. Efforts at finding positive models in Jesus and "the beloved disciple", Mary and Martha, David and Jonathan, etc. can only be judged as pathetic efforts at constructing a biblical warrant for homosexual practice where none exists. If Jesus or his followers had practiced or condoned homosexuality, it would have been profoundly scandalous within first-century Jewish culture.[112]

A more sophisticated type of argument in defense of homosexuality is offered by those who propose that acceptance of gay Christians

---

[112] The discussion of moving from then to now has been influenced by Richard Hayes' discussion in his book Moral Vision of the New Testament, pgs. 394-396.

in the twenty-first century church is analogous to the acceptance of Gentile Christians in the first century church. It is argued that Acts 10 and 11, the story of the Roman soldier Cornelius coming to Christ through the instrumentality of the Apostle Peter and the Holy Spirit, became a model for the Church to expand the boundaries of Christian fellowship by recognizing that God's Spirit had been poured out on those previously considered racially unclean and now can be appropriated to conclude that we must expand the boundaries of Christian fellowship to recognize that God's Spirit has been poured out on those heretofore considered sexually unclean! But is this an appropriate analogy? I think not. The Church did not simply observe the experience of Cornelius and his household and decide that the scriptures were wrong. No, the experience of Cornelius led Peter and the Church back to a new reading of Scripture. This new reading revealed a clear message of God's intent to bless the nations alluded to in Genesis 12:1-3, Deuteronomy 10:17-18, Psalm 15:1-2 and Amos 9:11,12, passages that illustrate that "God shows no partiality, but in every nation anyone who fears him and does what is right is acceptable to him" (Acts 10:34,35).

The new experience of the Spirit proved illuminating of Scripture (cf. Galatians and Romans) and caused the Jewish church, over time, to accept Gentiles into the church. This is precisely the step that has not been taken by the advocates of homosexuality in the church. Is it possible to reread the New Testament and show how the reality of married homosexuals who have the Spirit of God can be understood as a fulfillment of God's design for human sexuality as previously revealed in scripture? In view of the content of the Bible, I think not! I do not deny that married homosexuals who acknowledge Jesus as Lord may in fact possess the Spirit. Paul's letter to Corinth indicates that the Spirit regenerated believers and had given spiritual gifts to believers who were still committing sins and in need of repentance. This included sex with temple prostitutes (6:12-20), incest (5:1-8), arrogant discrimination in the eating of the Lord's supper (1 Corinthians 11:17-34), and several others. The fact that the Spirit lives in broken, worldly believers is not an occasion for self-congratulations but for repentance.

173

Fourthly, the mode in which the New Testament speaks explicitly about homosexuality is the mode of revealed reality, which creates a worldview. Romans 1:18-32 presents, as we have seen, a portrayal of human kind in rebellion against God and, consequently, plunged into depravity and confusion. In the course of that portrayal, homosexual activities are explicitly and without qualification identified as symptomatic of tragically confused rebellion. Romans 1 functions as a diagnostic tool describing God's glory, man's rebellion, God's wrathful "giving us up" and our resulting sins. Part of the diagnosis has to do with a dishonorable "exchange" of the natural for the unnatural.

To take the New Testament as authoritative in the mode in which it speaks is to accept this portrayal as "revealed reality", an authoritative disclosure of the truth about the human condition. Understood in this way, the text requires a comprehensive evaluation of homosexual practices as a distortion of God's order for creation.

Part of the "revealed reality" of Scripture is the picture of creation in Genesis 1 and 2. This passage was considered authoritative by Jesus when he was confronted with questions regarding divorce and remarriage in Matthew 19:1-9. Jesus clearly exalts Genesis 1 and 2 above Deuteronomy 24:1-2, declaring Deuteronomy 24:1 to have been written because of the hardness (meanness) of their hearts. Jesus said, "Haven't you read that at the beginning, the Creator made them male and female?" Jesus understood the vision of marriage within Genesis 1 and 2 to be authoritative for his disciples. He understood Deuteronomy 24:1 to have been an accommodation to Israel's sin. Therefore, Jesus did not consider Deuteronomy 24:1 to be authoritative for his disciples in the Kingdom.

The scriptures clearly teach us with commands in Leviticus, with principles in 1 Corinthians 6:20 and with negative models in 1 Corinthians 6:11. Clearly the revealed reality or worldview of God and sin in Romans 1:18-32 and the vision of heterosexual marriage in Genesis stand in opposition to homosexuality as a distortion of the created order. The vision of marriage in Genesis 1 and 2 is heterosexual and does not include homosexual relations. These commands, principles, models and revealed realities constitute the ways in which God speaks to us through scripture today.

I find no promise of God yet to be fulfilled nor any anticipation of God doing anything in the End Times that will supersede the scripture's diagnosis of homosexuality. Furthermore, I see the Cross, the Church and the Last Day's Spirit transforming the mind of the church from homophobia to agape – not in order to accommodate the gay lifestyle but to liberate. The church must be discipled and transformed to embody Jesus in all of her life. A part of that repentance will bring radical change in same-sex strugglers. We are called to love each other in our brokenness. This is what it means to live out our lives together in the Now and Not Yet of the End Times.

The fact that two same-sex people tell me they are "in love" with each other does not compel me to tear scriptures out of my bible for their sake. The comments, "I am in love with you, and I must live with you" or furthermore, "I must have intercourse with you" – married or not – are said millions of times a week by heterosexuals as well as homosexuals. These same people want a "loving" non-judgmental word from the church. These people need a hard, loving word of redeeming truth. What is at stake here is the biblical perspective. The Revisionist interpretative approach as already referenced is a hodgepodge of randomly selected Bible passages, Jesus, sin and experience.

COMPETING AUTHORITIES: TRADITION, REASON AND EXPERIENCE

Given the rules, principles, models and revealed realities of scripture as the forms of God's guidance on this matter, do we accept the authority of the New Testament text for today's church? The answer does not solve the embodiment issues in the church. But we cannot discuss embodiment until we decide what it is we are trying to embody!

Other than scripture, there are at least three other competing moral authorities. The scripture is weighed in relation to these three sources of moral wisdom: tradition, reason and experience. All of us read scripture through these lenses all the time. In our time, experience is the primary lens for most of us. Unfortunately, these authorities weigh at least as heavily as scripture on the minds of most church members.

Recently, I taught a class on homosexuality. I walked through the scriptural exegesis, the biblical theology behind the teachings, worked through the interpretive step of moving from then to now and finally discussed the Church's need to embody the scriptures teaching. A Christian psychiatrist friend of mine in the class began articulating his conviction that given the reality of "loving" same-sex relationships he knew about and the possible genetic factors involved, he believed the Church should approve of loving homo-sexual marriages. When he finished his statement I asked him, "By what spiritual authority outside of yourself do you hold this position?" He blinked, stuttered and said, "I have none and I have no need of one." His "spiritual" authority had no roots in scripture, the Holy Spirit or Jesus. His authority was his reason and his experiences! These authorities are for him countervailing authorities that far <u>outweigh</u> scripture.

This view of the nature of the Bible embraces the Enlightenment's three hundred year old trust in human reason and experience, with the fashionable evolutionary assumption that the present is wiser than the past. This position, now invading the Church, concludes that the world has the wisdom and the Church must play intellectual catch-up in each generation in order to survive. From this standpoint, everything in the Church becomes relative to the Church's evolving insights, which are determined by society's continuing development. The Holy Spirit is therefore relegated to merely helping the faithful see where the Bible doctrine is only reflective of the cultural limitations of the ancient world and the need to make adjustments in light of latter day experiences. In other words the Holy Spirit is identified with the spirit of the age. Same-sex unions are just one example.

It is crucial that we refuse to give human reason more authority than scriptural revelation. We also must certainly reject the evolutionary assumption that the present is wiser than the past. But is not the Holy Spirit working within the Church, illuminating today's church for the task of moving the scripture and her teachings into today's church? On issues such as war, slavery, role of women and homosexuality and so forth we are to listen for the leading of the Spirit. We have much more to learn from the Spirit and from Scripture. The Holy Spirit, however, is not the servant of the spirit of the age. The Spirit is not the lackey of human reason, corrupted by sin nor is it the slave of evolving cultural insights. Yet the Spirit is guiding believers to more faithfully apply the Scripture to the great moral issues of our time. The Spirit is leading us to more truth inside the confession, Jesus is Lord. The Spirit is not leading us to reinvent Jesus or the nature of the moral life.

Tradition. Although mainstream Judeo Christian tradition has been in opposition to homosexual practice since Day One, it has too often suffered from homophobia and from unbiblical hostility towards this particular sin. Tradition has not modeled the open liberation of those who struggle with same-sex sins. It desperately needs a transformation by the Spirit, as to the significance of the biblical teachings of creation, sin, the cross, new community and eschatology (Now and Not Yet). Tradition does not need transformation in order to excuse homosexual behavior, but to properly judge it and to openly and lovingly redeem it.

Reason. Some argue that since homosexuality is so widespread it must be moral. Can we make moral conclusions from statistics? There is widespread incidence of homosexual behavior, but the percentages of exclusive same-sex behavior is probably closer to 2.8 percent of men and 1.4 percent of women – not the well advertised 10 percent.[113] Even researchers find the results of scientific investigation inconclusive as to the issue of genetic predisposition towards homosexuality. Gay social issues are not characterized by reason but by politics and prejudice. It is not in the name of reason that we label people "homosexual" after one homosexual encounter! Rather, it is often because of the political agendas of the dismissive secular left and the homophobic religious right!

Is it scientific reason or political agendas that argues from inconclusive gene research that homosexual acts are not a choice but are genetically predetermined? Isn't "reason" trying to prove homosexual acts are not a choice so that gays will qualify as a discriminated against class such as African Americans or women? Political

---

[113] David G. Myer and Letha Scanzoni, What God Has Joined Together, (San Francisco, Harper, 2005), p. 55 for almost identical numbers.

agendas declare there are no ex-gays because homosexuals do not qualify as a legal class if there is a decision or a choice involved. There are thousands of people in this country who have experienced true healing from homosexuality. Are we to believe they are all liars or deceived? The "gay" community preaches a doctrine of fatalistic genetic determinism that has no basis in reality or reason.

What does reason do with the stories of men who were in the gay community eight or ten years ago who now father children and love their wives passionately? What good is reason if it prostitutes itself to an ungodly agenda? What good is reason when it suspicions all declarations of liberation? Should not reason, in this instance, be more enlightened and pragmatic? For example, why do we label people and discourage them from ever changing? We do this knowing that at best they will live very difficult lives as "gay people." Why not err on the side of redemption?

Experience. There are believers who live in loving homosexual relationships, just as there are heterosexual believers who live in loving relationships with their "significant other." There are heterosexual believers who have divorced their mates for no significant reason and who now live in "loving" relationships. All of these people claim the experience of grace – not the wrath – of God. How are their claims to be assured on the basis of their experience? Are such experiential claims simply another manifestation of the self-deception that Paul describes? Have new realities emerged since Paul? Does the practice Paul condemned in the ancient world correspond to the experience of homosexual relations that exist in the 21st century? For example, it is argued that Paul was concerned with pederasty (homosexual relations between an adult and a youth) which does not correspond to mutual loving relationships between two adults today, though the texts of Romans 1 and 1 Corinthians 6:11 are clearly not referring to pederasty.

I conclude that the experience of a believer or unbeliever does not supersede the authority of scripture. David enjoyed the adultery with Bathsheba. Incest was pleasurable to at least one member of the Corinthian Church as was temple prostitution. Abandoning our wives and marrying another after a "no-fault" divorce is experientially enjoyable. Pleasure almost always feels right! But even the experience of 'love" does not transform right into wrong and wrong into right. Our propensity for narcissistic self-deception remains legion. Experience is only a lens through which I look at the biblical texts.

Therefore, it is not only biblical but also prudent and necessary to let the unanimous testimony of scripture order the life of the Spirit-guided church. We must affirm that the scriptures tell us the truth about ourselves as sinners and as sexual creatures as well as the truth regarding the nature of covenant marriage between a man and a woman.

The answer to the original question, "How in the world can you put the authority of Scripture above tradition, reason and experience?" is not as simple as, "God said it. That settles it." This chapter has attempted to walk through the great issues we face as we move from then to now. We seek to hear the authoritative Word of God as revealed to the world through the person of Jesus Christ the Lord. As Christ's Disciples we see reason, tradition and experience as only lenses through which we look at truth, but we dare not make those lenses countervailing authorities within the life of today's Church. Only Jesus who is the Word of God is Lord!

DISCUSSION QUESTIONS

1. What is the significance of the collected Canon of Scripture for the life of the Church?
2. Discuss the authority of the rules, principles, models and revelations of reality (i.e. Cor.1, 2 and Romans 1:18-32) over your life.
3. We use reason to read scripture, but does reason have authority over revelation?
4. Discuss experience as a lens and/or as spiritual authority.
5. Discuss tradition as a lens and/or a spiritual authority.
6. What is the place of the Holy Spirit in the interpretation of scripture in the Church?

Afterword

The following testimonies testify to the power and presence of the Lord in His Body, the Church. These short statements of faith witness to the power of the Spirit within the New Family under God. These unfinished stories reach back fifteen or more years and walk on into a hopeful future of Kingdom surprises.

John

As a child I remember always feeling different from everyone else. I didn't' understand why. I just knew I was different. I didn't like the same things as other boys my age and when pressed by my Dad was incredibly resistant to doing "boy-like" things. Because of these feelings I had always struggled with feeling inferior and unloved by everyone, including God.

Even as a child I took solace in the community of believers. I always had a place there even though I felt as though I didn't exactly quite fit in. It wasn't perfect but it offered me love and acceptance that I couldn't get elsewhere.

As I went through adolescence and finally into young adulthood I realized and discovered that I was a homosexual. It wasn't something I didn't know but it was something that I wasn't ready to know until that time.

Once I realized what I was dealing with I tried to change but was doing it on my own recognizance, knowing my current church body would never be able to deal with it. I lived a homosexual lifestyle for a couple of years and finally moved to the city where I could really live "the life." I decided to get involved with a gay church and various gay organizations. Although this brought acceptance and justification in my choices I still did not feel complete in any way.

Eventually not satisfied with where I was, the Lord led me to a church body that understood the power of Jesus' healing blood. This was a group that accepted me but also helped me realize that God had a higher calling for me and that I was giving my heart and energy to something that really didn't glorify Him in any way.

I was involved with recovery groups, home churches and different aspects of the church body and everything I did helped to seal in my heart the overwhelming desire I had to serve God. It was in this body of believers that I discovered that God had a plan for me and that He loved me. Even when I was living a wholly sinful life He loved me.

Being a part of a community of believers offered me the chance to be accountable to people. They encouraged me to live my life honestly and openly so that all of the dark places in my heart could be exposed to the light.

The nature of my sin had also revealed that I need to be fathered. I loved my dad but early on in my life he was sent off to Vietnam. During that time I suffered abuse and decided that I would have nothing to do with my dad. I rejected him and anything he had to say about being a man. The men in the church body, particularly my home church, were wonderful in their willingness to father me and show me what it means to be a man of God.

The church is where I found that God desired for me to live a life different and better than I could have ever imagined. God's purposes were made known to me only because I found people who were willing to speak truth and life into my heart. They also helped prepare me for my beautiful wife, my son, my deep abiding friend-ships and a feeling that I had never understood before – love.

Michael P.

How has the church helped me define my view of what a real man is? The following church practices provided a foundation of trust that enabled me to reconstruct what a true Godly man is:

- Acceptance and love for me where I was at
- Seeing me for who I would become, not who I was trying to be at the time – a flat out refusal to allow me to define myself by my sin
- Willingness to become vulnerable with their own sins without making me the token sinner

Acceptance was huge for me. I wanted to be approved of and liked. Coming into the church with guilt and shame over my homosexual acting out only added to the tug-of-war going on inside of me over following God or running into the arms of another man. What I found at Lake Highlands was not what I expected. There was an acceptance of me as a person right away, whether they knew or guessed my past or not. I was not made to feel like my sin disqualified me from Jesus or from their friendship. This endeared me to Christ and to them, helping me build trust and confidence in the body of Christ. I soon found myself opening up and releasing years of pinned-up never discussed issues and sin that in turn brought freedom.

I had a desire for family but had resigned myself to never having a traditional family life. Lake Highlands had a true heart for family and especially father-lead and empowered families. There were weeks I came and sat in the pew weeping over the expressions of fatherly and brotherly love being played out before my eyes. I had never seen such open heterosexual affection between father and son or man to man. I was taken back and so desired to know, feel and understand this kind of love. I had substituted this with the act of sex with men for years. I had no idea of how to give or receive this kind of affection. I struggled to differentiate between right and wrong attitudes and emotions over love between men. The church embraced and enveloped me into the experience of redefining a

185

Godly masculine man. They encouraged me to live as that man as I was purposed to be by God.

The church walked me through this re-adolescence and would encourage and call out the truth along the way and when necessary would confront me about wanderings from the God created path. The church never once told me I could not have a family, but rather involved me in their families and lived out in front of me how to do family. I began to see parts created in me for marriage and masculine fathering that had never been exposed. I soon found myself realizing my created place in a traditional family setting.

The church also helped me reclaim my emotional and sensitive characteristics and marked them as masculine. My artistically talented abilities and career were also reclaimed from the homosexual stereotypes and given new freedom of expression. I soon found meaning, purpose and God design in the man that He had created. The place in the puzzle that I was trying to fit into was never meant for me in the first place. Right shape and color piece – wrong puzzle.

Real people living out real life – what a concept. If I hadn't have experienced this for myself I don't think that I would have believed it. The church was willing to be open with me about their own sin. As I started confessing, the church confessed right along side me. I found from this that I was not alone in the sin department. No, it may not have been the same sin, but it was real and hard and ugly. This released the shame and guilt. I was allowed to be real and not be torn down. It allowed me to focus on others and not myself, giving us all a place to real, accepted and burden lifted.

Dennis

I believe I have had a heart hungry for God since I was a boy, but because I grew up in a faith that did not model authenticity, weakness, or confession of sin, I had no where to go but inward with my struggle with homosexuality. It became my greatest fear that someone would find out my secret and reject me. I based all of my relationships on this belief, so I never got fully honest with anyone. I loved God and begged him to change me, but it was all in private. I did not overtly rebel as a teenager and hoped that my "good behavior" would sway God to answer my prayer.

I have always been very involved in church life, but as my struggle turned to addiction, a stark double life sprouted. Guilt and shame consumed me. I always resolved to "do better" and had "starting over" down to a weekly routine. I knew I had forgiveness in Christ, but I could not seem to find the power to live differently. I suppose what I really wanted was a "holy zap" so I could continue doing "great things for God" and never tell anyone what happened.

As a result of my sin addiction, I lost my job in 1995 as a youth minister at my church in Dallas. My greatest fear became my reality. Suddenly 600 people knew. I thought I might die or at the very least run far away. I never expected to be back in church six days after being fired. Immediately people began telling me their own confessions of sin. This was shocking. I had no experience with this kind of weakness in Christians! They begged me to stay to receive healing and restoration. This was unthinkable. Jim Reynolds called me to the front and exhorted the church to stand with me. This was real church. I decided to stick around.

My journey included a weekly home group and a Godly older woman in the church who taught me to hunger for God in everyday life. God was getting bigger. I also began meeting on a weekly basis with two men a few years older than me. For the first time in my life I began to tell the truth. They told the truth too, so I was not the identified patient or project of the group. This happened week after week for 10 years and I did not receive rejection! We also spent time together as friends outside our meeting time to run and even train for a marathon. I have lost count of the amount of hours we have spent together, but somewhere along the way, transformation began to happen.

My addiction was intense, so I did not let go of it easily. I had many falls, so the news each week was not always good, but no one left the room! One of the most intense days was after another confession of mine. My friends took me in the car to where I acted out on a frequent basis. In essence, they entered my hell. We talked and prayed there. No one had gotten this close. I was not in control and this was good. Light was shining on something I had protected for years. I shall never forget the impact of that day, though in the moment it was not pleasant.

God was finally able to show me the missing element of His beautiful powerful community. The rich relationships I had began to help me get a vision that marriage and family might be possible for me! I married my wife in 2000, and we had a daughter in 2004. My story is widely known in this church today. Miraculously I never left. This was the best decision I ever made. I returned to work on the staff in 2003 in an administrative role. This is not a trophy of any kind, but a sheer act of continued grace. Facing what I thought was my biggest fear, turned out to be the biggest blessing of my life.

Wesley

I think that every boy longs for a mentor, someone to lead him through life and help him become a man. For me, that longing was confusing because running along side this huge need that I couldn't express was this enormous guilt that I didn't dare express. That guilt and shame effectively kept me at arms length from the very thing I needed – male affirmation, friendship, touch and intimacy. I was different in a profound way, so I thought, and my homosexual feelings would forever be a barrier between me and "normal" boys and men. My guilt was birthed from my faith but there was no redemption, only conditional grace and despair.

To this day I wonder what my life would have been like had a Christian man mentored me earlier on in life through the feelings and emotions, guilt and shame, sin and questions that were in abundance, all of which I hid and stuffed away deep down inside. But praise God – it's never too late. And after years of false starts, disappointments and failures the Lord answered my prayers in the man and pastor, Jim Reynolds.

It is appropriate that I would call out his influence on my life among all the other divine influences the Lord has offered me throughout the years. I was 29 when we first met and for almost ten years he has been both friend and father, pastor and brother to me. He has hung with me through impossible times, times that would test the most patient of Christians. He offers me fellowship when I withdraw it. He pursues me when I run and receives me when I come crawling back. He holds me and offers me comforting touch, something I no longer am ashamed to ask for or seek from my Christian brothers. He models openness and transparency about both his sins and his faith. He has taught me how to have healthy arguments, how to be angry, how to grieve and how to be a man of integrity.

Having grown up in the church, one of my greatest fears was to be disfellowshiped. More specifically, it was to be caught in sin and to bring shame upon myself and on my family. As a result, I took great pains to punish myself before anyone else had a chance too. And I was good at it. No need to confess; I had condemned myself more severely and more resolutely than any judge possibly could and I had sentenced myself to time and hard labor without parole. A works based faith came easy to me and from an early age I had drawn the line that I would spend most of my adult life trying to balance. Fall beneath it into sin and be separated from God. Stay above it by works and hard labor and be in His good favor. The revelation, of course, was in discovering that God doesn't hang out above the line; He's only found beneath it. In fact, in Christ there really is no line. Quite the contrary: to draw a line of works is to separate one's self from Grace and from God.

So I spent the first five years with Jim and the Lake Highlands Church testing the waters. It was the hit and run method: spend 20 minutes on disclaimers, beat around the bush, and finally eek out something that remotely sounds like a confession and then run. Only no one there let me run, at least not far. It's hard to forget the night the men from my home church scaled the fence of my backyard to get to my house. They brought church to me that night and helped me shake off my shame. With these men I came to realize that quite frankly my sin was boring. They weren't flippant about it or insensitive but through their own confessions and the way in which they received mine they helped me believe that there was nothing special or shocking about my struggles. I was just one among many sheep in need of a shepherd. They gave me a loving environment that I came to trust in and gradually I started exposing more layers of my struggle sooner rather than later. And the best part was they didn't send me away, even when I tried to force their hand.

My journey with Christ in the Now and Not Yet is not complete, nor is my struggle with homosexuality. It has taken me a long time to overcome years of defense mechanisms and to say what I'm thinking and share what's really on my heart. It still scares me, but not nearly as much. Why? Because I know without a doubt that these people love me. They are invested in me and they absolutely will not give up on me. And a sign of my healing is that I feel the same way about them. No longer is my life my own to do with as I please. These people are my family and we bear one another's burdens just as readily as we rejoice in one another's good fortune. We are to one another nothing more and nothing less than the very embodiment of Christ himself. And we will spend the rest of our lives trying to comprehend the amazing mercy and grace of our God and Father that binds us together in love.

Thank you, Jim. Thank you for imparting your wisdom and faith so freely into me. Thank you for this book and for the tireless and extensive research that went into writing it. And most importantly, thank you for your tender and compassionate heart from which all this springs.

Printed in the United States
127111LV00008B/247-264/A

9 781602 669338